The Human Condition

THE HUMAN CONDITION

Lewis Worrow

Contents

The Long-Term Mating Strategies of Men 34

Foreword

In the history of western civilization, the scientific study of human sexual behaviour has received very little attention. What little attention it did receive was not good: Plato denigrated it, arguing that it should lead to something better or higher (SEE: *Phaedrus*, *Symposium*), Aristotle barely mentioned it, and Christian philosophers condemned it: Augustine argued that its pleasures are dangerous in mastering us, and allowed sex only for procreation (*City of God, Book 14; On Marriage and Concupiscence*), while Aquinas confined its permissibility to conjugal, procreative acts (*Summa Theologia, Book III; Summa contra Gentiles*). Immanuel Kant (*Lectures on Ethics*) considered it the only inclination that cannot satisfy the Categorical Imperative, and Jean-Paul Sartre claimed that sexual desire aims to capture the other's freedom (*Being and Nothingness, Part III, Chapter 3*). Only during contemporary times do philosophers, beginning with Bertrand Russell (1929) and including Sigmund Freud (1905), think of sex as generally good.

Sex raises fascinating issues. Rooted in our biology, pervaded by our intentionality, and directed at other human beings, sexual desire is complex and not confined to specific mating seasons. Its pleasures are powerful and have ruined many lives. Men and women seem to exhibit, desire, and experience sex differently. Why this is so is debatable, but these issues make it crucial to understand sexual desire, pleasure, activity, and preferences, and to explore the moral aspects of sex.

First Principles of Evolutionary Psychology

Adaptations

Adaptation is the evolutionary process where an organism becomes better suited to its habitat. It is a process that takes place over many generations. Adaptations are thus inherited and are reliably developed characteristics that come into existence through natural selection as a result of them helping solve problems of survival or reproduction. Adaptations that persist usually do so as a result of being better than alternative designs existing in the population during the period of their evolution; for example, the umbilical cord.

Adaptations must have genes "for" for the adaptation, however. Those genes are required for the passage of the adaptation from parents to children; hence, adaptations have a genetic basis. Of course, most adaptations cannot be traced to a single gene but rather are the products of many genes.

Adaptive Unconscious

The adaptive unconscious is a set of unconscious mental processes influencing judgment and decision making. It is different from conscious processing: that is to say, it is much faster, effortless, and much more focused on the present. It is the interpreting of information and response to said information conducted very quickly and outside the conscious view.

Evidence for the existence of the adaptive unconscious comes by way of case studies and experiments; for example, the ventromedial area of the cerebral cortex is a small bit at the front behind the nose and is responsible for sifting through the copious amount of information we receive from the external world, prioritising it and flagging things which require our immediate attention. When Damasio studied patients who had damage to this area of the brain, it was found that people with damage to this area were still as rational and as intelligent as before but lacked judgement and found it very difficult to make decisions. Another factor that has been shown to degrade decision making is confusion caused by too much unorganised information which we term as "analysis paralysis."

By-products

By-products are characteristics that do not solve adaptive problems and do not have functional design; they are "carried along," so to speak, with characteristics that do have functional design because they do happen to be coupled with those adaptations; example: the belly button.

Costs of Adaptation

Adaptations are never perfect. There are always trade-offs between the various functions and structures in a body and all adaptations come with a price. Selection pressures, therefore, pull in different directions, and the adaptation that results is some kind of compromise; for example, the peacock's ornamental train reduces his ability to camouflage, fly and even manoeuvre, but affords him advantages in terms of sexual selection.

Dominant Gene

Dominance, in genetics, is said to be completely genetically dominant over another when it is expressed equally in the homozygous and heterozygous conditions; for example, a mother has brown hair but has genes for both brown and red hair. Her mate also has the genes for brown and red hair. This means that each parent would each have a chance of passing either brown or red hair genes to their children meaning their offspring could have either brown or red hair. Thus, a person might look different from their parents but look like their grandparents or great grandparents.

Envy

Envy is one of the least studied emotions in ethology, but it is extraordinarily important. As we know it, envy is linked to status in that people experience it when someone else has mates, prestige, property, or resources that they want to, but fail to, possess. Speaking functionally, it motivates us to imitate those who have been successful in getting what they want, be it in the form of hero worship or idealization, in a positive manifestation of the emotions of envy. On the negative side, envy prompts us to take actions that tear down those who have more than we do, such as derogating their achievements; for example, a husband might degrade his wife's achievements to maintain his dominant position in the marriage.

Typically, women tend to experience envy of rivals who are more physically attractive than they are, whereas men tend to experience more envy of rivals who have more sexual experience and more attractive mates.

Evolution

Evolution is a biological process. It is how living things change over time and how new species develop. The theory of evolution explains how evolution works and how living and extinct things have come to be the way they are. More formally, the theory of evolution is composed of three essential ingredients: differential reproductive success, inheritance, and variation.

To become an ancestor of future generations, an organism must reproduce. Thus, the possession of traits that increases or decreases an organism's chances of surviving and reproducing is the "bottom line" of evolution by way of natural selection. The traits of organisms that reproduce more than others, therefore, get passed down to future generations at a relatively greater frequency.

Milestones in Human Evolutionary History

Time	Event
15 Billion Years Ago (BYA)	The Big Bang
4.7 BYA	Earth Forms
3.7 BYA	First Life Emerges
2.5 BYA	First Organism to Use Oxygen
1.2 BYA	Sexual Reproduction Evolves
500-450 Million Years Ago (MYA)	First Vertebrates
365 MYA	Fish Evolve Lungs and Walk on Land
248–208 MYA	First Mammals and Dinosaurs Evolve
208–65 MYA	Large Dinosaurs Flourish
114 MYA	Placental Mammals Evolve
85 MYA	First Primates Evolve
65 MYA	Dinosaurs Go Extinct
35 MYA	First Apes Evolve
8–6 MYA	Ancestors of Humans Evolve
4.4 MYA	Primates Evolve Bipedal Locomotion
3 MYA	Australopithecines Evolve in Africa
2.5 MYA	Invention of Oldowan
1.8 MYA	Hominids Spread to Asia
1.6 MYA	Evidence of Fire (Likely Hearths)
1.5 MYA	Invention of Acheulean Hand Axe
1.2 MYA	Brain Expansion in Homo Line Begins
1.0 MYA	Hominids Spread to Europe
800 Thousand Years Ago (KYA)	Crude Stone Tool Kits Used
600–400 KYA	Evidence of Hunting Spear
500-100 KYA	Rapid Brain Expansion in Homo Line
200–300 KYA	Neanderthals Flourish in Eurasia
150-120 KYA	The ancestor of All Humans Evolves
150-100 KYA	Evidence of Complex Speech
140 KYA	Evidence of Long-Distance Trade
110 KYA	Evidence of Beads and Jewellery
100-50 KYA	Exodus from Africa
50 KYA	Evidence of Clothing and Ritual Burial
50-35 KYA	Explosion of Art, Fireplaces and Tools
40-35 KYA	Homo sapiens Arrive in Europe
30 KYA	Neanderthals Go Extinct
12 KYA	Hominids Spread to Americas
10 KYA	Evidence of Agricultural
5 KYA	Evidence of Writing
Present	Homo sapiens Colonise Entire Planet

Evolutionarily Stable Strategy

An evolutionarily stable strategy (ESS) is a strategy that is impermeable when adopted by a finite population in adaptation to a specific environment. That is to say, "if all the members of a population adopt it, no mutant strategy can invade" (John Maynard Smith, 1982). It is a refined or modified form of a Nash equilibrium that holds if all players adopt their respective parts, no player can benefit by switching to any alternative strategy.

Fisher's Principle

Though not the originator of the idea, Fisher would provide us with an evolutionary model which explains why the sex ratio of most species that produce offspring through sexual reproduction is approximately 1:1 between males and females. He posited that the parental expenditure of both sexes is equal as a result of each sex supplying precisely half the genes of all future generations.

If we were to imagine that male births are less common than female births and that, as a result, a new-born male now has better mating prospects than a new-born female, then we could also expect the new-born male would go on to have more grandchildren. Therefore, parents who are genetically dispossessed to producing males would tend to gain an advantage, as they have an increased number of grandchildren born to them. If this is true, then ultimately the genes responsible for male-producing tendencies would spread, and male birth would become more common until eventually the sex ratio approached 1:1 and the advantage associated with producing males dies away.

Fitness

Fitness is the relative ability of an organism to survive and pass on its genes to the next generation. It is usually equal to the proportion of the individual's genes in all the genes of the next generation. Simply put, if differences in individual genotypes affect fitness, then the frequencies of the genotypes will change over generations; the genotypes with higher fitness become more common.

However, Hamilton reasoned that classical fitness was all but too narrow in its account of natural selection and failed to emphasise groups of genes rather than individuals. He hypothesised that the fitness of an organism is also increased to the extent that its close relatives also reproduce. This is because relatives share genes in proportion to their relationship and thus natural selection must favour characteristics that cause an organisms' genes to be passed on regardless of whether an organism produces offspring directly.

Fixed Action Patterns

Animals with nervous systems are born with instincts. One such set of instincts are fixed action patterns, in which a very short to medium length sequence of actions, without variation, are carried out in response to a clearly defined stimulus.

They are stereotypical behavioural sequences that an animal follows after being triggered by a well-defined stimulus. Once a fixed action pattern is triggered, the animal will perform it to completion; for example: showing a certain male duck, say, a plastic facsimile of a female duck or such alike will trigger a rigid sequence of courting behaviour.

Founder Effect

Founder effect describes the effects on a population's subsequent evolution directly attributable to the fact that founder individuals of the colonizing population have only a small, and probably non-representative, sample of the parent population's gene pool. Subsequently, evolution may take a different course from that of the parent population as a result of this limited genetic variation. In extreme cases, founder effects result in the new population ultimately being distinctively different from the parent population, both genotypically and phenotypically, and consequently become a new species.

Game Theory

Originating as an application of the mathematical theory of games in a biological context, evolutionary game theory provides a framework of contests, strategies, and analytics by which Darwinian competition can be modelled. Paradoxically, as Smith notes, "it has turned out that game theory is more readily applied to biology than to the field of economic behaviour for which it was originally designed."

Nash Equilibrium

Nash equilibriums are a concept within game theory where the optimal outcome of a game is one where no player has an incentive to deviate from their chosen strategy after considering an opponent's choice. Imagine a game between two players – Player α and Player β. In this simple two-player game, both players choose a strategy of either (i) to receive £1 or (ii) to lose £1. Logically, both players should choose to receive £1.

If you revealed Player α's strategy to Player β and vice versa, it would be hard to conceive of either player deviating from their chosen strategy. Simply knowing the other player's move does not materially change either player's behaviour. Therefore, outcome AA below represents a Nash equilibrium.

		Player α	
		A	B
Player β	A	1, 1	1, -1
	B	-1, 1	0, 0

Genes

Genes are forms of DNA (a collection of chemical information that carries the instructions for making the proteins a cell will need) and humans have about 20,000 genes that code proteins, and many more that are non-coding. Genes are the smallest discrete units that are inherited by offspring intact, without being broken up or blended.

Mendel, Darwin's contemporary, is credited with accounting for how animals and plants passed on traits, something Darwin was unable to do with his theory of natural selection. Involving more than 30,000 pea plants spanning eight generations, he speculated that inheritance was "particulate" and not, as had been believed at the time, blended. His work showed that the qualities of parents were passed on, intact, to their offspring.

He published his work in 1866, demonstrating the actions of invisible "factors" (genes) and their predictability in determining the traits of an organism, but it would take more than three decades for his laws to be rediscovered. Today, he is known as the "father of modern genetics".

Genetic Bottlenecks

A genetic bottleneck, or population bottleneck, is a sharp reduction in the size of a population due to environmental events such as disease, droughts, earthquakes, famines, fires, floods, and human activities, such as human population planning and speciocide.

Such events can reduce the variation in the gene pool of a population. Thereafter, a smaller population, with a smaller genetic diversity, remains to pass on genes to future generations of offspring through sexual reproduction. Consequently, the allelic frequencies may have been considerably altered and thereby affect the future evolution of the species irrevocably; for example, the catastrophic eruption of Vesuvius which devastated Herculaneum and Pompeii.

Genetic Drift

Where there is a significant statistical change in gene frequencies resulting not from emigration, immigration, or natural selection, but instead as a result of causes operating randomly concerning the finesses of the alleles concerned, genetic drift is said to have occurred.

Genetic drift may cause gene variants to disappear completely and thereby reduce genetic variation; however, is thought to only occur and be of significance in a small population. It can also cause initially rare alleles to become much more frequent and even fixed.

Genotype

The genotype is the genetic constitution of an organism, mainly its genome. The extent to which the genotype influences the phenotype varies hugely. Some aspects of the phenotype are almost entirely determined by heredities, such as blood types and eye colours.

However, in the case of human language, things are more technical. Our capacity to learn and speak a language may be said to be inherited, but which language is spoken is entirely learnt and is thus environmental.

Imprint

Imprinting is any kind of phase-sensitive learning that is rapid and independent of the consequences of behaviour.

First observed in the 10th-century by amateur biologist Spalding, and later rediscovered by the biologist Heinroth, imprinting is a form of "preprogrammed" coding into certain animals' biology to affix their attention on the first object with which it has an auditory, tactile, or visual experience; example: ducklings imprint on the first moving object they observe. Typically, in nature, this would be their mother, but if the first object a duckling sees is a human leg, it will follow that person instead.

Instinct

Instinct, when properly defined, describes well-outlined acts whose causation is inherited only, and which are triggered by specific stimuli called "releasers." In the animal kingdom, it accounts for innate behaviour chains such as courtship, fighting and the building of nests to name a few. That said, any behaviour is instinctive if it is performed without being based upon prior experience, that is, in the absence of learning; for example, sea turtles, newly hatched on a beach, will instinctively move toward the ocean, and automatically swim when they are in the water.

Intersexual Selection

Intersexual selection, or mate choice, occurs when females choose between male mates based on a form of consensus. Traits selected by male combatants are called secondary sexual characteristics (including antlers and horns), while traits selected by mate choice are called "ornaments". Consequently, those who lack the necessary "weapons" to get the best of another in combat fail to mate and thus fail to become ancestors.

Therefore, evolutionary change occurs simply because the qualities that are desired in a mate increase in frequency with the passing of each generation who have desirable traits; example: if females prefer to mate with males who give them food or gifts, then males with qualities that lead to success in acquiring food and gifts will increase in frequency over time.

Intrasexual Selection

Intrasexual competition occurs between two members of the same species that compete for the opportunity to mate with a female; for example, two stags locking horns in combat wherein the victor gains access to a female either directly, or through controlling territory or resources desired by the female.

This prototype of intrasexual competition highlights well that whatever qualities lead to success in the same-sex contest, such as athletic ability, size or strength will be passed on to the next generation because of the mating success of the victors. Inversely, those qualities that are linked with losing, fail to get passed on resulting in change over time simply as a consequence of intrasexual competition.

Sexually dimorphic traits, size, sex ratio, and the social situation may all play a role in the phenomena's male-male competition has on the reproductive success of a male and the mate choice of a female. Larger males tend to win male-male conflicts due to their sheer strength and ability to ward off other males from taking over their females.

Mutation

A mutation is an alteration in the nucleotide sequence of the genome of an organism and is the product of copying errors in a piece of DNA. Although most mutations hinder survival or reproduction, some, by chance alone, end up helping the organism in greater numbers. If the mutation is helpful enough to give the organism a reproductive advantage over other members of the population, it will be passed down to the next generation in greater numbers. Over many generations, if it continues to be successful, the mutation will spread to the entire population so that every member of the species will have it.

Take, for example, the genetic mutation which affected the OCA2 gene in our chromosomes some 6,000 - 10,000 years ago resulting in the creation of a "switch" of sorts that quite literally "turned off" the ability to produce brown eyes. This event occurred in a single individual who today is the common ancestor of all peoples with blue eyes.

Natural Selection

Natural selection is the process where organisms with favourable traits are more likely to reproduce. In doing so, they pass on these traits to the next generation. Over time this process allows organisms to adapt to their environment. This is because the frequency of genes for favourable traits increases in the population.

Nature

All species have their unique nature. This is captured in the qualities that define them, each having a unique adaptation that differs from those of other species; for example: take the humble hedgehog, porcupine, and skunk, all of which defend themselves against predators but each doing so in a different way.

It is part of the male lion's nature to walk on four legs, grow a large furry mane and hunt other animals for food, just as much as it is the butterfly's nature to enter a flightless pupa state, wrap itself in a cocoon and emerge to soar gracefully in search of food and mates.

Each species, after all, is the product of adapting to somewhat unique selection pressures throughout evolutionary history and has therefore had to face different adaptive problems.

Noise

Noise is the random effects produced by forces such as chance mutations, sudden and unprecedented change in the environment or even change effects during development; for example, the particular shape of a person's belly button.

Sometimes, these random effects can cause functional operational failures. Some even argue that the mental disorder known as schizophrenia can be traced back to a high mutation load that causes random effects which disrupt normal psychological functioning. However, in most cases, such random effects are materially harmless and simply imperfections.

Parental Investment Theory

Parental investment theory, a term coined by Trivers in 1972, predicts that the sex which invests more in its offspring is, in turn, also the sex that will be more selective when it comes to choosing a mate. Consequently, the sex which invests less in its offspring will also be the sex that will engage in intrasexual competition for access to mates.

Trivers later extended parental investment theory in 1974 to include an account of the parent-offspring conflict, an impasse that arises out of a conflict of interests of what the parent deems optimal as an investment versus the offspring's perspective.

Phenotype

The phenotype of an organism is the whole set of traits of that organism. Phenotypes are determined mainly by genes and are influenced by environmental factors. So, knowing the genome of an organism does not give an exact prediction of its phenotype.

The interaction between genotype and phenotype has often been conceptualized by the following relationship:

genotype + environment → phenotype

Pride

Pride appears to be an emotion that motivates people to perform actions that are highly valued by others, to advertise those actions publicly, and thereby increase a person's status and respect in the eyes of others. Pride emerges early in life and has been observed across all cultures. It is activated when a person's accomplishments and achievements are publicly recognised and thereafter continues to serve as a motivational function in terms of motivating people to strive to achieve socially visible accomplishments and also to advertise said achievements to others. Not coincidentally, displays of pride have been confirmed to be attractive in the mating arena across four continents and 16 cultures so far.

Rage

Rage is a hypothesised reaction to the loss of status. Rage may function to motivate an individual to seek revenge on the person who caused the status loss and represents that rage, and the consequent revenge that sometimes takes place following the said loss of status is justified retaliatory aggression.

Recessive Gene

Recessive, in genetics is said to be completely recessive to dominance and is only expressed in homozygous conditions unless paired in heterozygous conditions with a less recessive gene; example; of a set of parents, a mother only has genes for brown hair and the father only the genes for red hair. In this instance, the child will inherit the genes for red hair and brown hair. As the brown hair gene is dominant over the red hair gene this means the child will have brown hair even though she has genes for both brown and red hair. This means only one dominant gene is needed for the child to receive that particular trait, while two recessive genes are needed for one.

Sexual Selection

Sexual selection is a special kind of natural selection. Traits selected by mate choice are called "ornaments." Females often prefer to mate with males with external ornaments – exaggerated features of morphology. Genes that enable males to develop impressive ornaments or fighting ability may simply show off greater disease resistance or a more efficient metabolism. This idea is known as the "good genes" hypothesis.

Sexy Son Hypothesis

The "sexy son" hypothesis proposes that a female's optimal mate choice from an array of potential mates is the one whose genes are best suited for producing male offspring who possesses the best chance of reproductive success. Consequently, such a proposition inherently implies that the other benefits that a mate could offer (nuptial gifts, parental investment, territory, etc.) are of diminished importance than first appear. Where her "sexy son's" future breeding success is concerned, the more successful they are at producing offspring, the more likely they are to produce offspring who carry copies of her genes.

Weatherhead and Robertson are credited with devising the hypothesis in 1979. However, before this, Dawkins had noted that "in a society where males compete with each other to be chosen as he-men by females, one of the best things a mother can do for her genes is to make a son who will turn out in his turn to be an attractive he-man. If she can ensure that her son is one of the fortunate few males who wins most of the copulations in society when he grows up, she will have an enormous number of grandchildren. The result of this is that one of the most desirable qualities a male can have in the eyes of a female is, quite simply, sexual attractiveness itself."

Zygosity

Organisms whose cells have a nucleus enclosed within a nuclear envelope (Eukaryotes) possess two identical sets of chromosomes; that is to say, they are diploid. Diploid organisms, such as ourselves, by extension, have the same loci on each of their two sets of homologous chromosomes, except that the sequence at these loci may differ between said chromosomes in a matching pair and that a few chromosomes may be "mismatched" as a result of a chromosomal sex-termination system. However, as the DNA sequence of a gene often varies from one individual to another (what we term as alleles), zygosity is employed as a measure of defining the degree of whether two alleles have identical or different DNA sequences.

The words homozygous, heterozygous, hemizygous and nullizygous are used to define the genotype of any given diploid organism at the level of a single locus on the DNA. Where both alleles of a diploid organism are the same, we may say the organism is homozygous at the locus. Where the alleles of a diploid organism are different, such an organism may be said to be heterozygous at the locus.

Where one allele is missing, it is hemizygous and, if both alleles are missing, it is nullizygous.

The Long-Term Mating Strategies of Men

BMI, Fat, and Waist-Hip Ratio

Female physical attractiveness encompasses body mass proportion, facial symmetry, mid-upper arm circumference, waist-hip ratio, and youth; all of which provide cues to a women's reproductive capacity. However, no single definition of physical attractiveness gives a complete account, as physical attractiveness means different things to different people and different human cultures. The Bushmen of Australia, Kenyans, and Ugandans prize plumpness, for example, as it signals adequate nutrition during development, health, and wealth. In cultures where food is abundant, such as in the United States and many Western European countries, the wealthy distinguish themselves by being slim.

Additionally, one potential universally attractive quality may be a low waist-hip ratio. Healthy, reproductively capable women typically have waist-hip ratios of between 0.67 and 0.80. Those with higher waist-hip ratios, on average, have more difficulty becoming pregnant, and those who do get pregnant do so at a later age than women with lower ratios. One study conducted even found that women with a low waist-hip ratio and relatively large breasts, compared to women from three groups with different combinations of body-shape variables, had 26% higher levels of the ovarian hormone oestradiol (E2), which is a good predictor of fertility and pregnancy success (Jasienska, Ziomkiewicz, Ellison, Lipson, and Thune, 2004).

Commitment and Marriage

Commitment between individual people is like a social contract. In ancestral times, a commitment was often a prerequisite to copulation. Failure to commit often meant failing to become an ancestor. For those men that did commit, they were afforded a multitude of advantages which modern men share in too. These benefits include, but are not limited to, the following nine powerfully adaptive benefits: (i) increased odds of succeeding in attracting a mate, (ii) increased ability to attract a more desirable mate, (iii) increased paternity certainty, (iv) increased survival of his children, (v) increased reproductive success of children accrued through parental investment, (vi) increased social status, (vii) added coalition allies, (viii) access to his partner's resources and status and (ix) increased lifespan.

Contrast Effects

Contrasts are the difference you find when you compare something or someone. Contrast effects are consequentially the enhancement or diminishment, relative to normal perceptions, as a result of successive or simultaneous exposure to comparative stimuli. They are an unconscious bias that occurs in response to two things being judged relative to one another as opposed to individually.

Men carry with them the same evaluative mechanisms that evolved in ancient times to induce men to consider switching mates and decrease their commitment to their existing mate. However, the potential dangers of modern life mean that these mechanisms are artificially activated by the dozens of attractive women we witness daily in our advertisement-rich society on billboards, in magazines, in movies, on TV and websites result in the exploitation of men's' mating psychology. Women too are adversely affected as a result of forming unhealthy standards by which to contrast themselves against. Research conducted in the early nineties found that groups of men who looked at photographs of highly attractive women would later report their attraction to their current partner as lessened (Kenrick, Neuberg, Zierk, and Krones, 1994). They also felt less close to, less committed to, less satisfied with and less serious about their actual partners.

Necessities and Luxuries

Necessities and luxuries permeate modern purchasing decisions with most of us spending more of our money on the necessities of life such as food. However, as one's "budget" increases, most people would spend more on luxuries. These economic concepts also apply to the domain of mate preference. This raises the question of what people prefer when they have a low versus a high budget of "mating currency," a concept that corresponds to mate value.

The budget allocation method goes some way to answer this question. Li and his colleagues gave participants in a study varying budgets - low, medium, and high. They discovered that when given a low budget men allocated a relatively large proportion of their budget to physical attractiveness whereas women allocated a relatively large proportion of their budget to resources. As the budget increased, both men and women spend an increasing proportion of their allowances on "luxuries" such as creativity, intelligence, kindness, and liveliness. These findings parallel individual differences in mate value: those low in mate value have less choice, so they want to ensure adequate levels on the necessities of mating. As mate value increases, people can afford to be choosier on a wider array of characteristics.

Paternity Uncertainty

The human female is rare among primates in as far as possessing the queer adaptation of concealed or cryptic ovulation. Concealed ovulation obscures a women's current reproductive status and dramatically changes the ground rules of human mating. Men now find women attractive throughout the ovulatory cycle, not just during ovulation. This creates a particular adaptive problem for men by decreasing the certainty of their paternity. Whereas with primate males who only need to prevent other males from mating with their mate for a brief period during which she is in estrus, the human male must always be on guard. In contrast to human males then, the male primate can be fairly confident of his paternity as he only needs to sequester and have sex with her during a sharply constrained period. Before and after her estrus, he can go about finding food and solving other adaptive problems without running the risk that his partner will become impregnated by another male if she is unfaithful.

To solve this problem ancestral men sought qualities in a potential mate that might increase the odds of securing their paternity: (i) the desire for premarital chastity and (ii) the quest for post-marital sexual fidelity. On the assumption that a women's proclivities towards chaste behaviour would be stable over time, her premarital chastity would signal her likely future fidelity. A man who did not select a chaste mate ran the risk of investing in a woman who would cuckold him. Not uncoincidentally, men place a premium on virgin brides more so than women value virgin grooms, at least in the United States, according to at least one cross-generational mating study. However, the value men place on virginity has been declining in line with the increasing rate of readily available birth control though not uniformly across the world (Buss et al., 2001); example: people in China, India, Indonesia, Iran, Palestinian Arab areas of Israel and Taiwan attach a high value to chastity whereas people in Finland, France, Germany, Norway, Sweden and the Netherlands hold that virginity is large if not wholly irrelevant when it comes to selecting a mate.

Positions of Power

Men with resources and status, qualities that women desire in a long-term mate, are better able than men without status and resources to translate their preferences for young attractive women into actual mating behaviour. Men high in occupational status tend to marry women considerably more physically attractive than men low in occupational status. Men are even aware of their ability to attract more desirable women.

Grammer's study of 2,638 Germans found that as men's income goes up, they seek younger partners (Grammer, 1992). Not dissimilarly, it was also found that men who are high in mate value express a stronger preference for facially feminine women than those who are less attractive (Burriss, Welling, and Puts, 2011).

Sex Differences in the Importance of Physical Attractiveness

Because of the abundance of cues conveyed by a woman's physical appearance, and because male standards of beauty have evolved to correspond to these cues, men place great importance on physical appearance in their mate preferences. However, the importance people place on attractiveness is not fixed. The importance of attractiveness has dramatically increased in modern times regardless of cultural living arrangements, ethnicity, habitat, hemisphere, location, marriage system, mating system, political system, race or religion (Buss and Schmitt, 1993).

Men's preference for physically attractive mates appears to be the product of a species-wide psychological adaption that transcends cultural variation, after all, men have consistently rated good looks and physical attractiveness as more important to them than women have in studies dating back to 1939.

Sperm Competition Theory

Sperm competition theory provides an account for variations in sperm insemination. The number of sperm inseminated into a female by a mate is directly linked to the odds of conceiving offspring. Sperm may find themselves in competition with the sperm from another male and so it holds that probability favours the male inseminating more sperm. In a study to determine the effect of sperm production of separating mates from each other, 35 couples agreed to provide ejaculates resulting from sexual intercourse using condoms. The partners had been separated for varying intervals of time. Men's sperms went up dramatically with the increasing amount of time the couple had been apart since their last sexual encounter. When the couples spent 100% of their time together, men on average inseminated 389 million sperm per ejaculate. But when the couple spent 5% of their time together, men inseminated 712 million sperm per ejaculate. The more time spent apart, the more sperm the partners inseminated in their mates when they finally did have sex regardless of the time since the man's last ejaculation.

The authors of the study rightly concluded that the number of sperm inseminated increases when other men's sperm might be inside their mate's reproductive tract at the same time due to the opportunity provided for extramarital sex. The increase in sperm inseminated by the male after prolonged separation could reasonably be assumed to increase the odds that it will be his sperm that succeeds in racing to the egg by crowding out or displacing a possible interloper's sperm.

Standards of Beauty

The content of men's' mate preferences is, in many ways, similar to those of women. Both sexes express a desire for partners who are healthy, intelligent, kind and understanding. Intelligent long-term mates, after all, offer an abundance of benefits that aid in solving mutually relevant problems of survival such as childrearing, skill in navigating social hierarchies and even good genes that can be transmitted to children. Kind and understanding partners tend to be empathetic, good at social "mind-reading" and highly cooperative in the relationship.

Therefore, individuals who select healthy mates to benefit from their ability to thrive in adverse circumstances, remain energetic in accomplishing the tasks of everyday living and pass on such genes for doing so to their children. Those who seek a mate who possess such qualities and who are similar to them in attitude, personality and religious beliefs are more likely to maximise their odds of long-term cooperation in the course of their mate-ship and reduce conflict.

However, where men differ is in their preferences for standards of physical beauty. Female attractiveness has evolved to embody reliably observable cues to fertility or reproductive value and these standards of beauty emerge quite early in life, with infants as young as two to three months old gazing longer at attractive faces than their less attractive counterparts (Langlois, Roggman, and Reiser-Danner, 1990). Consequently, it seems no training seems necessary for these standards to emerge, and this is consistent with findings that standards of beauty span across cultures regardless of culture or degree of exposure to media. Features of physical appearances, such as body fat distribution, clear eyes, clear skin, full lips, good muscle tone, lustrous hair and smooth skin and features of behaviour, such as animated facial expressions, a bouncy, youthful gait and high levels of energy are all physical cues to health and youth, and hence fertility and reproductive value, and are key components of male standards of female beauty. But why would this be? Because it is precisely these preferences that solved the adaptive problem of selecting a reproductively healthy mate. Chief among these cues to a woman's reproductive status – her age.

Testosterone

Testosterone ($C^{19}H^{28}O^{2}$), or T, is an androgen sex hormone and plays a key role in the male mating effort, the time and energy devoted to besting same-sex competitors and pursuing mates. Higher T-levels facilitate the male pursuit of females, with T-levels increasing after interacting with attractive women (Roney, Mahler, and Maestripieri, 2003).

However, maintaining high T-levels is costly. Doing so can compromise immune functioning and, because it is linked with mating effort, it may interfere with parenting effort. Consequently, it is thought by evolutionists that T-levels should drop after a man succeeds in attracting a long-term mate, and studies have found exactly this (Burnham et all., 2003; Gray et al., 2004). One study even found that men in committed relationships had T-levels that were 23% lower than their unpaired counterparts. Another still found that men in long-term relationships (defined here as being more than 12 months) had substantially lower T-levels than their single counterparts or men in a newly formed relationship (Farrelly, Owens, Elliott, Walden, and Wetherell, 2015). Notably, the lowest T-levels of all belong to married men who had children.

The Hunting Hypothesis

It is common knowledge that ancestral methods of securing food have been linked to the rapid emergence of modern humans. What is lesser known is the importance of hunting in human evolution. Hunting as we know it was majorly important to our evolution and is a much-debated topic amongst anthropology, evolutionary biology and evolutionary psychology. One widely held view is that the model of "man the hunter" (Tooby and Devore, 1987). According to this view, the transition from mere foraging to large-game hunting provided a major impetus for human evolution, with a cascading set of consequences including a rapid expansion of toolmaking, tool use and the development of a large human brain, and the evolution of complex language and symbolism necessary for communication and cooperative hunts.

The Provisioning Hypothesis

Proponents of the hunting hypothesis argue that it can explain a large number of unusual features of human evolution (Tooby and Devore, 1987). Most importantly, it can account for the fact that human males are unique among primates in terms of their heavy parental investment in children. This has been called the provisioning hypothesis.

Because meat is an economical and concentrated food resource, it can be transported efficiently back to the home base to feed the young. In contrast, it is far less efficient to transport low-calorie food over a long distance. Hunting, therefore, provides a plausible explanation for the emergence of the heavy investment and provisioning that men channel towards their children.

The Show-Off Hypothesis

Hunting produces resources that are unique among the food groups in two respects: (i) meat comes in large packets, sometimes more than the hunter and his immediate kin can consume, and (ii) the packages are unpredictable. Two consecutive kills of large game animals in a week could be followed by a long period of hunting failure (Hawkes, O'Connell and Blurton Jones, 2001a, 2001b). These qualities establish the conditions for the sharing of meat beyond the confines of one's immediate family and these periodic abundances would become known to everyone in the community (Hawkes, 1991).

Hakes thusly proposed the show-off hypothesis, suggesting that women would prefer to have neighbours who are show-offs – men who go for the rare but valuable abundance of meat – because they benefit by gaining a portion of it. Women, after all, stand to gain from these gifts, especially in times of shortage, and so it is to their advantage to reward men who pursue showing-off. They could welcome back good hunters with favourable treatment, such as siding with them in times of dispute, providing health care to their children and offering sexual favour.

Consequently, men who pursue the risky hunting strategy would therefore benefit in several ways: by gaining increased sexual access to women, they increase their odds of fathering more children. The favoured treatment of their children by women from neighbours increases their survival and increases their odds of reproductive success.

An analysis of data from a study of five hunter-gatherer societies – Ache of Paraguay, Hadza of the East African savanna, Kung of Botswana and Namibia, Lamalera of the Indonesian Island of Lembeta, Meriam of Australia – concluded that the better hunters typically enjoyed having more desirable mates, more mates on average and higher rates of offspring survival (Smith, 2004).

Women's Fertility and Women's Reproductive Value

Reproductive value refers to the number of children a person of a given age and sex is likely to have in the future. A woman who is 19 years of age, for example, has a materially higher value than a woman who is 39 because, on average, the younger woman is likely to bear more children. However, the 19-year-old might decide never to have children and the 39-year-old could have triplets. The key is that reproductive value refers to the average expected future reproduction of a person of a given age and sex.

Reproductive value differs from fertility, a word which is here defined as actual reproductive performance measured by the number of viable offspring produced. In human populations, women in their mid-20s tend to produce the most viable children, and so fertility among humans reaches its peak in the mid-20s.

Youth Preference

Youth preference is an evolutionarily essential strategy. A woman's youth is the chief indicator of her reproductive value for as a woman steadily moves past age 20, her reproductive value declines until at age 50 it is approximately zero. Youth preference then is, unsurprisingly, uniformly expressed by men. Men, on average, desire a mate who is younger than they are, and this preference is not limited to Western cultures with

Indian, Indonesian, Iranian and Nigerian men all having been observed in displaying this similar preference. An exception to this rule is teenage boys who prefer slightly older women because slightly older women have higher fertility than women their age or women who are younger (Kenrick, Keefe, Gabrielidis, and Cornelius, 1996).

The Long-Term Mating Strategies of Women

Ambition and Industriousness

Among all the tactics for getting ahead in everyday life, sheer hard work proves to be one of the best predictors of historic and potential income generation. Those who work hard reap the rewards of higher levels of education, promotions, salaries and status compared to their lazy and unmotivated peers (Jencks, 1979; Willerman, 1979; Kyl-Heku and Buss, 1996; Lund, Tamnes, Moestue, Buss, and Vollrath, 2007).

In most cultures then, it is not surprising that women value ambition and industriousness more so than men do, typically rating them as between important and indispensable. Cross-cultural and cross-historic evidence supports the key evolutionary psychological prediction that women have evolved a preference for men possessing signs of the ability to acquire resources and are far less attracted to men lacking the ambition one needs to secure resources and success.

Athletic Prowess, Formidability and Height

The importance of physical characteristics in the female choice of a mate is notable throughout the animal world. Male gladiator frogs are responsible for creating nests and defending the eggs. In most courtships, a stationary male gladiator frog is deliberately "bumped" by a female who is considering him. She will strike at him with great force, sometimes enough to scare him away. If the male moves too much or bolts from the nest, the female hastily leaves to find a more enduring alternative mate. This process aids the female frogs in assessing how successful the male will be at defending her clutch. This "bump test" then reveals the male's physical ability to protect her and her offspring.

Human beings do not perform such a bump test, but the preference for athletic prowess, formidability and height manifest all the same. Take the baboons residing in the savanna plains of Africa, in which studies by primatologist Barbara Smuts found females frequently formed "special friendships" with males provided they offered physical protection to them and their infants in exchange for sexual access (Smuts, 1985).

Like primates, human women who form long-term mateships benefit from the physical protection a man can offer. A male's athletic ability, physical prowess, size and strength are all indicative cues that signal solutions to the problem of protection. In Britain and Sri Lanka specifically, women have a strong preference for male physiques that are lean and muscular (Dixon, Halliwell, East, Wignarajah, and Anderson, 2003).

Women also often judge short men, for example, to be undesirable for either a short-term or a long-term mate (Buss and Schmitt, 1993). Generally, women find it very desirable for a potential marriage partner to be athletic, physically strong and tall. Tall men specifically are consistently seen as more desirable as dates and mates than are short or average-height men, with two studies finding that among women, 80% preferred men six feet or taller (Cameron, Oskamp, and Sparks, 1978).

Choice Copying (Copycatting)

When a person's attraction to or choice of a potential mate is influenced by the preferences and mating decisions of others, this phenomenon is called choice copying or copycatting. It has been documented and observed across several species ranging from birds to fish, and now in humans.

Two studies independently found that women judged a man to be more attractive when he was surrounded by women, compared to when he was standing alone (Hill and Buss, 2008a; Dunn and Doria, 2010). Incidentally, two other studies found that a distinctive mate copying effect presented itself when the man being evaluated was paired with a physically attractive woman (Waynforth, 2007; Little, Burriss, Jones, DeBruine and Caldwell, 2008). However, the effect is most profound when women believe that the man is partnered with the singular woman, inferring that he possesses unobservable qualities that women prize in a potential mate (Rodeheffer et all, 2016). Taken together, these studies reveal that women use social information in mate selecting and put simply, a man being paired with attractive and interested women is an important clue to his desirability as a mate.

Dependability and Stability

Among the 18 characteristics rated in Buss's worldwide study on mate selection, the second-and third-most-highly-valued characteristics were a dependable character and emotional stability or maturity. In fact, in 21 out of 37 cultures, men and women had the same preference for dependability in a partner (Buss et al., 1990). Of the remaining 16 cultures, women in 15 valued dependability more so than men, rating a dependable character as 2.69, where a 3 signified indispensable; men rated it nearly as important, with an average of 2.50.

In the case of emotional maturity and stability, the sexes differ more greatly. Women in 23 cultures valued this quality significantly more than did men; in the remaining 14 cultures, men and women valued emotional stability equally. Averaging across all cultures, women gave such a quality a 2.68, whereas men gave it a 2.47.

These characteristics may thus possess great value to women worldwide for two reasons. Firstly, they are reliable signals that resources will be provided consistently over time. Secondly, men who lacked such dependability and emotional stability prove often to act erratically and inflict heavy emotional and other costs on their mates (Buss, 1991). They tend to monopolise shared resources and act self-centred. More than this, they show higher-than-average sexual jealousy, becoming enraged when their wives merely talk with someone else. They are overly dependent on others fulfilling their needs. They are emotionally, physically, and verbally more abusive. They have more affairs than average, suggesting further diversions in resources and time. All of this is so to say that those lacking in such qualities cost too much and endanger being able to solve problems critical to adaptation.

Economic Resources

Choosing a mate is a complex task, and so we do not expect to find simple answers to what women want. However, the evolution of the female preference for males offering resources may be the most ancient and pervasive basis for female choice in the animal kingdom.

Among humans, the evolution of women's preferences for a long-term mate with resources would have required two preconditions. Firstly, resources would have to be accruable, controllable, and defensible by men during human evolutionary history. Secondly, men would have to differ from each other in their holding and their willingness to invest those holdings in a woman and her children.

Throughout human history, it has been observed that some women garner more resources for their children through a single spouse than through several casual sex partners. Men invest in their children and wives with provisions to an extent unprecedented among primates. Whereas in all other primate species, females are almost exclusively self-sufficient when it comes to acquiring food, rarely is this the case in humans (Smuts, 1995). Human men males provide food, shelter, and territory to defend and protect their families. They tutor children in athletic passions, friendship, hierarchy, negotiation, and social influence. They transfer status, aiding offspring in forming reciprocal alliances later in life. These benefits are unlike anything offered by other primate males.

It is no wonder then that when the stage was set for the evolution of women's preferences to favour men with resources. But women needed cues to signal a man's possession of those resources. These cues might be direct or indirect, but the possession of economic resources provides the most obvious clue of all.

Adaptive Problems and Hypothesized Solutions

Adaptive Problem	Evolved Mate Preference
Selecting Mates Able to Invest	Ambition/Industriousness
	Good Financial Prospects
	Size, Strength and Athletic Ability
	Slightly Older Age
	Social Status
Selecting Mates Able to Parent Well	Dependability
	Emotional Stability
	Kindness
	Positive Interactions with Children
Selecting Mates Able to Protect	Athletic Ability
	Bravery
	Masculine Body Type
	Size (Height)
Selecting a Healthy Mate	Health
	Masculine Features
	Physical Attractiveness
	Symmetry
Selecting Mates Willing to Invest	Dependability and Stability
	Love and Commitment Cues
	Positive Interactions with Children
Selecting a Mate Who is Compatible	Similar Ages
	Similar Personalities
	Similar Values

Evolved Psychological Mechanisms

Men differ in their, ambition, athletic skill, emotional stability, empathy, industriousness, intelligence, kin network, kindness, physical prowess, position in the status hierarchy, sense of humour and social skills. Men also differ concerning the cost they carry into a mating relationship: some come with children, some with debt, others with a bad temper or selfish disposition, but all come with a cost. Men differ in hundreds, if not thousands, of ways that may be irrelevant to women. From among these, selection over hundreds of thousands of years has focused and refined women's preferences with laser-like precision upon the most adaptively valuable characteristics.

That is not to say that such valuable characteristics are by any means static. On the contrary, because the challenges to survival change over time, so do the contents of women's preferences. Those seeking a mate must gauge the future potential of a prospective partner. A man might lack resources now, but, as a law student, might he have excellent future promise? Those choosing a mate must look beyond moment-to-moment positions and speculate a mate's future potential.

In short, evolution has favoured and rewarded women who prefer men possession attributes that confer benefits and who dislike men possession attributes that impose costs. Each separate attribute constitutes one component of a man's mate value to a woman as a mate. Each of her preferences tracks a single critical component. In selecting a mate then, women must deal with the problem of correctly evaluating the cues that signal whether a man possesses a particular quality. The assessment problem becomes especially acute in areas in which men are apt at deceiving women, such as pretending they have greater status than they do or feigning greater commitment than they are truly willing to give.

Her evolved psychological mechanisms will also face the problem of balancing and integrating the knowledge they possess regarding a prospective mate. Suppose one man is emotional unstable but extremely generous, another emotionally stable but unwilling to share. Which man should a woman choose? Selecting a mate requires psychological mechanism that make it possible to add up the relevant attributes and give each a weighted value in her final decision.

Good Financial Prospects

Currently held mate preferences provide a window for viewing our mating past, just as our fears of spiders or snakes provide a window for viewing ancestral hazards. Evidence from a litany of studies documents modern western women indeed value economic resources in mates substantially more than their male counterparts.

In a study conducted in 1939, for example, U.S men and women rated 18 characteristics for their relative desirability in a marriage partner, ranging from irrelevant to indispensable. Women did not view good financial prospects as indispensable, but they did rate them as important, whereas men rated them as merely desirable but not very important. Women in 1939 values good financial prospects in a mate then about twice as much as men did, a finding that was replicated in 1956 and again in 1967 (Buss, Shackelford, Kirkpatrick, and Larsen, 2001).

High Social Status

Traditional hunter-gatherer societies, one rough guide to what ancestral conditions were probably like but by no means the only one, suggest that ancestral men had clearly defined status hierarchies. Resources in most status hierarchies flow freely to those at the top and trickle slowly down to those at the bottom (Betzig, 1986; Brown and Chia-Yun, (n.d.)).

Cross-culturally, groups such as the early Egyptians, Indonesians, Japanese, Melanesians, and Sumerians all include people described as "big men" or "head men" who wield great power and enjoy the privileges of prestige. Among various South Asian languages, for example, the term "big man" is found in several Dravidian languages, Hindi, and Sanskrit. In Hindi, for example, "bara asami" means "great man" or someone high in rank. This is true of many cultures, many of whom have found it important to carve out and invent phrases or words to describe men who are high in status.

Men then who command a high position because of social status possess a universal cue to the control of resources, a much-desired trait of women. Along with status comes better food, more abundant territory and superior health care. It grants greater social status to children too and affords them social opportunities missed by the children of lower-ranking males. For male children worldwide, access to more and better-quality mates typically accompanies families of higher social status. One study of 186 societies, for instance, found that from the Mbuti Pygmies of Africa to the Aleut of Alaska, high-status men invariably had greater wealth and more wives and provided better nourishment for their children (Betzig, 1986).

Women then appear to have solved the adaptive problem of acquiring resources in part by preferring men who are high in status. Indeed, when forced to trade among different mate characteristics, women prioritise social status, viewing it as a "necessity" than a "luxury" (Li, 2007). Women evaluate men who possess high-status items such as luxury high-prestige cars and luxury apartments as especially attractive potential partners (Dunn and Searle, 2010; Dunn and Hill, 2014).

Incest Avoidance

Incest avoidance is one of the most important preferences that women avoid or find intolerable in a mate. Reproducing with genetic relatives is known to create "inbreeding depression," offspring with lower intelligence and more health problems because of the expression of deleterious recessive genes. Humans have powerful incest-avoidance mechanisms, such as the emotion of disgust at the thought of passionately kissing or having sex with a sibling (Lieberman et al., 2003; Fessler and Navarrete, 2004). Growing up with a sibling is a key cue that activates the inbreeding-avoidance adaptation (Lieberman, Tooby, and Cosmides, 2007; Lieberman, 2009). Indeed, co-residence duration predicts sexual aversions to peers with whom one grows up (Lieberman and Lobel, 2012). These incest-avoidance mechanisms are stronger in women than in men, which is consistent with parental investment theory – given that women have a greater obligatory parental investment in offspring, the costs of making a poor mating decision are typically higher for women than for men. Indeed, the characteristic "is my sibling" is one of the most powerful "deal breakers" for women when considering a potential mate, right up there with "beats me up" and will have sex with other people regularly when he is with me" and "is addicted to drugs" (Burkett and Cosmides, 2006). Other such deal breakers include, but are not limited to, being already married or in a relationship, dating multiple partners or being untrustworthy (Jonason, Garcia, Webster, Li, and Fisher, 2015).

Kindness, Humour and Voice

Women's desires are more complex than we could have ever imagined, and discoveries are being made every year. Women greatly value the traits of altruism, generosity and kindness in a long-term mate (Phillips, Barnard, Ferguson, and Reader, 2008; Barclay, 2010). The 37-culture study by Buss in 1990 found "kind and understanding" was universally ranked as the most desirable quality in a long-term mate out of 13 ranked qualities (Buss et al., 1990).

Barclay (2010) experimentally manipulated vignettes that differed only in the presence or absence of hints of altruistic tendencies. Women strongly preferred men with altruistic tendencies as long-term mates. Kindness towards whom matters, however. Women find kindness to be especially desirable when the kind acts are directed towards themselves, their friends and their family; they shift their preferences to lower levels of kindness when the kinds of acts are directed toward other targets such as other women (Lukaszewski and Roney, 2010). Kindness and altruistic proclivities signal the possession of abundant resources (Miller, 2007), the willingness to provide resources to a woman (Buss, 2016b), good character (Barclay 2010), good parenting and partnering qualities (Tessman, 1995; Buss and Shackelford, 2008) and a co-operative and non-cost inflicting disposition (Buss, 2006).

Women prefer long-term mates who have a good sense of humour too (Buss and Barnes, 1986; Miller, 2000). Humour has many facets, that we know, two of which being humour appreciation and humour creation. In long-term mating, women prefer and find attractive men who produce humour, whereas men prefer women who are receptive to the humour they produce (Bressley, Martin, and Balshine, 2006).

Why this is no one knows for sure, but one theory proposes that humour is an indicator of "good genes" (a fitness indicator), signalling creativity and excellent functioning of complex cognitive skills are not impaired by a high mutation load (Miller, 2000). Other research indicates that humour is used to indicate interest in initiating and maintaining social relationships (Li et al., 2009).

Women also find a deep voice especially attractive in a potential mate with a deep voice is well documented to be attractive in part because (i) it may indicate sexual maturity, (ii) larger body size or physical formidability, (iii) good genetic quality, (iv) dominance, and/or (v) all the above. For these reasons, it may be unsurprising to some to learn that men with attractive-sounding voices have sexual intercourse earlier and have a larger number of sex partners. These findings, along with direct evidence that women prefer men with a low voice pitch, mainly in casual sex partners, suggests that this preference is more central to short-term rather than long-term mating (Puts, 2005).

Older Men

The age of a man provides an important clue to his access to resources, and it does not go unnoticed. Just as it is true that young male baboons must mature first before they can enter the upper echelons of baboon social hierarchy, male human adolescents rarely command status and the respect of their peers before less they are mature men.

Older men have had more time to accrue and develop important alliances, cultivate skills, and learn more about the environment and how to navigate it – all beneficial attributes. The age-resources link reaches extremes among the Tiwi, for example, who is an aboriginal tribe located on two islands off the coast of northern Australia (Hart and Pilling, 1960). The Tiwi are a gerontocracy. meaning the oldest of men wield most of the power and prestige and even control the mating system through complex social alliances.

Averaged over all cultures, women prefer men who are between 2 and 3.5 years older than them, depending on the study. French Canadian women, who seek husbands just a shade under 2 years older are starkly different from Iranian women who seek husbands more than 5 years older. Why do women prefer somewhat older men, but not much older men? The answer seems to be that it is not the men in and of themselves, but the problems that develop in much older men. They are more likely to be infertile, less likely to live as long and so children are likely to suffer more genetic abnormalities and garner less investment from their father. However, somewhat elder men are likely to be reaping the benefits of the time they have spent investing in social alliances and acquired status – qualities directly beneficial to a woman and her children that can aid in their survival and their future mating opportunities.

Similarity and Homogamy

Successful long-term mating requires sustained co-operative alliances over time. Similarity, then, leads to emotional bonding, co-operation, communication, mating happiness, lower risk of breaking up and possibly increased survival of children (Buss, 2003; Castro, Hattori, and Lopes, 2012).

Men and women alike show strong preferences for mates who share their intellectual level, personal characteristics, political orientations, values and worldviews. This preference for similarity carries through into actual mating decision making, a phenomenon known as homogamy: people who are similar on these characteristics date and get married more often than those who are dissimilar (Wilson, Cousins, and Fink, 2006). Homogamy is strongest for intelligence, political orientation and religiosity. It is positive, but not strong for personality characteristics, including manipulativeness and narcissism (Kardum, Hudek-Knezevic, Schmitt, and Covic, 2017).

Homogamy for physical appearance, it has been hypothesised, might be due to "sexual imprinting" on the opposite-sex parent during childhood (Bereczkei, Gyuris, and Weisfeld, 2004). Interestingly, daughters who received more emotional support from their fathers were more likely to choose similar-looking mates (Watkins et al., 2011; Nojo, Tamura and Ihara, 2012). Finally, there is strong homogamy for overall "mate value", with the "10s" mating with other "10s" and the "6s" mating with other "6s" (Figueredo et all., 2015).

Symmetry and Masculinity

Mating with someone who is unhealthy would have posed several adaptive risks for our ancestors: (i) an unhealthy mate would have a higher risk of becoming debilitated, thus failing to deliver whatever adaptive benefits that might otherwise have been provided such as food, health care, investment in childrearing and protection; (ii) an unhealthy mate would be at greater risk of dying prematurely, thereby cutting off the flow of resources and forcing the search for a new mate; (iii) an unhealthy mate might transfer communicable diseases; (iv) and unhealthy mate might infect the children of the union, imperilling their chances of surviving and reproducing and (v), if healthy is partly heritable, a person who chooses an unhealthy mate would risk passing on genes for poor health to children.

For all these reasons, men and women both place a premium on the health of a potential mate. In a study of 27 cultures, on a scale from 0 (irrelevant) to +3 (indispensable), men (who gave it a rating of +2.31) and women (who gave it a rating of +2.28) both judged "good health" to be highly important (Buss et al., 1990).

Temporal Contexts

Mateship can last a lifetime, or, more commonly, be of a shorter dimension. In The Short-Term Mating Strategies of the Sexes, we will explore short-term mating in detail, but it is worthwhile to highlight in this section the findings that show that women's preferences shift as a function of temporal contexts.

Schmitt and Buss in 1993 asked women to rate 67 characteristics on their desirability in short-term and long-term mates. The rating scale ranged from -3 (extremely undesirable) to +3 (extremely desirable). Women found the following qualities to be more desirable in long-term marriage contexts than in short-term sexual contexts: "understanding" (average rating, 2.93 in long term versus 2.10 in short-term), "fond of children" (2.93 versus 1.21), "kind" (2.88 versus 2.50), "devoted to you" (2.80 versus 0.90), "responsible" (2.75 versus 1.75), "ambitious and career-oriented" (2.45 versus 1.04), "co-operative" (2.41 versus 1.47), "college-educated" (2.38 versus 1.05) and "creative" (1.90 versus 1.29).

These findings suggest that temporal context matters a great deal for women, causing shifts in their preferences depending on whether a casual sex partner or a marriage partner is sought (Schmitt and Buss, 1996).

The Gathering Hypothesis

In stark contrast to the view that it was men who provided the critical evolutionary impetus for the emergence of modern humans comes an opposing view. This hypothesis, the gathering hypothesis, suggests that women provided the critical impetus not through hunting as is suggested men did, but through gathering (Tanner and Zihlman, 1976; Zihlman, 1981; Tanner, 1983).

According to this hypothesis, stone tools were invented and used not for hunting purposes but instead for digging up and gathering various plants. The gathering hypothesis also goes on to explain that the transition from forests to savanna woodlands and grasslands were as a result of the use of tools that made securing gathered food more efficient and economical (Tanner, 1983).

After the invention of stone tools for gathering came the invention of containers to hold the food and the elaboration of tools for butchering, hunting and skinning animals. According to then to the gathering hypothesis, securing plant food with stone tools provided the primary evolutionary impetus for the emergence of modern humans. According to this view, it would seem, hunting came sometime later and did not play a key role in the emergence of modern humans.

This hypothesis provides a useful corrective to the exclusive focus that has been placed on male hunting in the evolution of humans and helps account for the fact that the diet of our primate relatives, and hence likely our pre hominid ancestors, consisted mainly of plant food. It also goes further in accounting for the fact that more than 35% of the diets of modern hunter-gatherers consist of gathered plant foods (Marlowe, 2005).

Women's Mate Value

A woman's physical attractiveness and youth are two indicators of her mate value or overall desirability to men (this we have already discussed above). Consequently, women who are young and more physically attractive have more numerous mating options and so can become choosier in their selections. But does a woman's mate value influence her mate preference? As you may have come to expect, the answer is yes.

Little and his colleagues had 71 women self-rate themselves on their perceptions of their physical attractiveness and subsequently showed them photos of men's faces that varied along the masculinity-femininity dimension. What he found has that women's attraction to masculine faces was significantly linked to the perception they held of themselves (Little, Penton-Voak, Burt, and Perrett, 2002). Furthermore, women who viewed themselves as physically attractive also showed a pronounced preference for symmetrical male faces (Feinberg et al., 2006) and men who displayed vocal masculinity, marked by a low-pitched voice (Pisanski and Feinberg, 2013).

The Short-Term Mating Strategies of the Sexes

Extramarital Affairs

An affair may be regarded as any passionate attachment, sexual relationship or romantic friendship between two people where at least one of the two has a connection with a third person, typically either in a marriage or relationship, without the third person's agreement or knowledge.

A romantic affair, which is also sometimes called an affair of the heart, maybe about the sexual actions of a more emotional relationship between two people who may have sex without expecting a more formal romantic relationship.

Men in most cultures pursue such extramarital affairs more often than do their wives. The Kinsey study, for example, estimated that 50% of men had extramarital affairs, whereas only 26% of women had them (Kinsey, Pomeroy, and Martin, 1948, 1953). The anthropologist Gregor described the sexual feelings of Amazonian Mehinaku men in this way: "Women's sexual attractiveness varies from 'flavourless' (*mana*) to the 'delicious' (*awirintya*)" (Gregor, 1985, 84). He further noted that "sad to say, sex with spouses is said to be mana, in contrast with sex with lovers, which is nearly always awirintyapa" (Gregor, 1985, 72).

Kinsey sums it up best: "There seems to be no question but that the human male would be promiscuous in his choice of sexual partners throughout the whole of his life if there were no social restrictions. The human female is much less interested in the variety of partners" (Kinsey et al., 1948, 589).

Genetic Benefit Hypothesis

Genetic benefits are a class of benefits whose advantages seem most obvious. The first being enhanced fertility: if a woman's regular mate is impotent or infertile, a short-term mate might provide a fertility backup to aid in conception. The second, albeit slightly less obvious benefit, is that a short-term mate might also provide superior genes compared with a woman's regular mate, especially if she has an affair with a healthy and/or high-status man.

In securing this better class of genes, her offspring may have better chances of survival or reproduction (Smith, 1984). One version of this is known as the sexy son hypothesis which we have spoken about already above in the first section of this book. In doing so, we observed that by mating with an especially attractive man, a woman might be able to bear a son who is also especially attractive to women in the next generation.

Thirdly, short-term mates might provide women with different genes compared with those of her regular mate, thus enhancing the genetic diversity of her children. A natural hedge, some might say, to mitigate against risks such as environmental change or disease.

Good Genes Hypothesis

The economics of the mating market suggests that, on average, women can secure superior genes from a short-term affair partner relative to her regular partner. After all, highly desirable men are often willing to have a brief encounter with less desirable women so long as they do not burden them with entangling commitments.

But what are they looking for in a short-term affair partner? The answer is heritable and honest markets of fitness and health that signal the presence of genes that facilitate resistance to environmental insults and diseases as exhibited by symmetrical men. Why symmetrical men you ask? Because symmetrical men, compared to their more lopsided peers, tended to be more likely to have sexual relations with women who were already in relationships (Gangestad and Thornhill, 1997). That is, women appear to be choosing symmetrical men as affair partners precisely because of their good genes and their disposition towards short-term mating.

Women also seem to place a great premium on physical attractiveness and desirability to other women. For casual sex, after all, women do prefer men who are confident, daring, humorous, strong and successful with attractive women (Kruger, Fisher, and Jobling, 2003). Not coincidentally, women also prefer short-term mating partners who possess masculine facial architecture (Waynforth, Delwadia, and Camm, 2005); who are muscular (Sacco, Young, Brown, Bernstein, and Hugenberg, 2012) and have darker limbal rings (Brown and Sacco, 2018), all of which indicate women look for honest signals of good genes and health cues.

Hook-Up Behaviour and Friends with Benefits

A wealth of behavioural evidence comes from studies of hooking up and friends with benefits. "Hooking up" typically refers to spontaneous sexual interactions in which the participants are not in a traditional romantic relationship and there is no explicit promise of any future intimate relationship (Garcia and Reiber, 2008). "Friends with benefits," in contrast, typically refers to a blend of traditional friendship with the "benefits" referring to having sex, but with no implied commitment to a romantic relationship (Owen and Fincham, 2010).

More men than women try to initiate hooking up (Garcia and Reiber, 2008) and are more likely than women to report having at least one friend with benefits. Although both women and men engage in these forms of sexual activity, their motivation for doing so appears to differ. Men, more than women, report that their "ideal outcome" of hooking up is "further hook-ups." Women, on the other hand, report that their "ideal outcome" would be a "traditional romantic relationship." This finding might explain why more men than women report friends with benefits, although the means must be identical for the sexes, men are more likely to construe a particular relationship as a friend with benefits, whereas women may perceive it as the early stage of a romantic relationship. Women also report feelings of more regret, feelings of being "used," and depression following hook-ups or one-night stands (Campbell, 2008).

Mate Preferences

The relaxation of standards does not mean that men have no standards. On the contrary, the standards that men do hold for casual sex reveal a precise and well-attuned strategy to gain a variety of partners. Compared with their long-term preferences, for casual sex that is, men dislike conservative women, have a low sex drive and are prudish (Buss and Schmitt, 1993). Men value sexual experience in a potential sex partner, reflecting a belief that experienced women are more sexually accessible. A high sex drive, sexual experience and proclivity for promiscuity are cues that a woman is of an increased likelihood of successful short-term mating. A low sex drive and prudishness, in contrast, signal difficulty in gaining sexual access and thus interfere with men's short-term sexual strategy.

Evolutionary psychologists have also hypothesized that men seeking short-term sex would prioritise women's bodies since body cues provide possibly the most powerful cues to her fertility (Currie and Little, 2009; Confer et al., 2010). In one experiment, participants viewed an image of an opposite-sex individual whose face was occluded by a "face box" and whose body was occluded by a "body box" (Confer et al., 2010). Participants then were instructed to imagine themselves having either a one-night stand or a committed relationship with the person and were then asked to decide on which box they would remove to inform their decision - they could only remove one box. Compared to the long-term mating context, in which men prioritised facial information, men considering casual sex shifted significantly in the direction of prioritising body information - a finding also discovered by Currie and Little (2009) using a different methodology. Women, in contrast, do not show this shift and tend to prioritise a man's face in both the short-term and the long-term mating contexts. These findings are consistent with the hypothesis that men prioritise cues to fertility in short-term sex partners.

Mate Switching Hypothesis

Sometimes, a woman's husband starts abusing her, stops bringing in resources, or otherwise declines in his value to her as a mate (Smith, 1984, Betzig, 1989; Fisher, 1992). Ancestral women might have benefited from short-term mating to cope with this adaptive problem.

There are several variants of this hypothesis, however. According to the mate expulsion hypothesis, having a short-term affair would help the woman to get rid of her long-term mate. Because men in many cultures often divorce wives who have affairs (Betzig, 1989), having an affair would be an effective means for the woman to initiate a breakup. Another variant of this hypothesis suggests that a woman might simply find a man who is better than her husband and so initiate a short-term encounter as a means of "trading up" to a higher-quality mate (Buss, Goetz, Duntley, Asao, and Conroy-Beam, 2017).

Orgasms

The physiology of women's orgasm provides one clue to an evolutionary history of short-term mating. Once it was thought that a woman's orgasm functioned to make her sleepy and keep her reclined, thereby decreasing the likelihood that sperm would flow out and increasing the likelihood she would conceive. But, if the function of orgasm were to keep the woman reclined to delay flowback, then more sperm would be retained. That is not the case: there is no link between the timing of the flowback and the number of sperm retained (Baker and Bellis, 1995).

Women discharge roughly 35% of sperm within 30 minutes of the time of insemination, averaged across all instances of intercourse. However, if the woman has an orgasm, she retains 70% of the sperm, ejecting only 30%. This 5% difference is not large, but if it occurred repeatedly, in woman after woman, generation after generation, it could add up to a large selection pressure over evolutionary time. Lack of an orgasm leads to the ejection of more sperm. This evidence is consistent with the hypothesis that a woman's orgasm functions to draw the sperm from the vagina into the cervical canal and uterus, increasing the probability of conception (Puts et al., 2012).

The number of sperm a woman retains is also linked with whether she is having an affair. Women time their adulterous liaisons in a way that is reproductively detrimental to their husbands. In a nationwide sex survey of 3,679 women in Britain, all women recorded their menstrual cycles as well as the timing of their copulations with their husbands and, if they were having affairs, with their lovers. It turned out that women having affairs time their copulations, most likely unconsciously, to coincide with the point in their menstrual cycle when they were most likely to be ovulating and hence were most likely to conceive (Baker and Bellis, 1995). Furthermore, women who are having affairs are more likely to be orgasmic with their affair partner than with their regular partner (Buss, 2016 b). Other studies find that women are especially likely to experience sexual orgasm with men who are masculine and physically attractive - qualities women typically desire in short-term mating (Puts, Welling, Burriss, and Dawood, 2012).

Prostitution

Prostitution, the relatively indiscriminate exchange of sexual services for economic profit, is another reflection of men's greater desire for casual sex (Symons, 1979). Prostitution occurs in every society that has been thoroughly studied, from the Azande in Africa to the Zuni in North America (Burley and Symanski, 1981).

Within the United States, estimates of the number of active prostitutes range from 100,000 to 500,000. Addis Ababa in Ethiopia has more than 80,000 prostitutes, Tokyo

130,000 prostitutes and Poland 230,000. In Germany, there are 50,000 legally registered prostitutes and triple that number working illegally.

In all cultures, men are overwhelmingly the consumers. Kinsey found that 69% of American men had solicited a prostitute, and for 15%, prostitution was a regular sexual outlet. The numbers for women were so low that they were not even reported as a percentage of the sexual outlet of women (Kinsey et al., 1948, 1953).

Resource Hypothesis

One benefit of short-term mating that cannot be overstated is resource accrual (Symons, 1979). Women could engage in short-term mating in exchange for goods meat or services. An ancestral woman might have been able to obscure the actual paternity of her offspring through several short-term matings and thus elicit resources from two or more men (Hrdy, 1981).

According to this paternity confusion hypothesis, each man might be willing to offer some investment in the woman's children on the speculative chance that they are genetically his own.   Another possible resource is protection (Smith, 1984; Smuts, 1985). Men typically protect their mates and children, including defence against predators and aggressive men. Because a primary mate cannot always be around to defend and protect a woman, she might gain added protection by consorting with another man.

Finally, Smith (1984) proposed the status-enhancement hypothesis of short-term mating. A woman might be able to elevate her social standing among her peers or gain access to a higher social circle by a temporary liaison with a high-status man. Women might gain a variety of tangible and intangible resources through short-term mating.

Sexual Desires, Fantasies, and the Sex Drive

Sexual fantasies provide psychological clues to the evolutionary history of men's proclivity to casual mating. They reveal the nature of desires that motivate men's and women's behaviours. Studies document large differences between male and female sexual fantasies.

Research, for example, conducted in Great Britain, Japan and the United States showed that men have roughly twice as many sexual fantasies as women (Wilson, 1987; Ellis and Symons, 1990). When asleep, men are more likely than women to dream about sexual events. Men's sexual fantasies more often include anonymous partners, multiple partners, or strangers. During a single fantasy episode, most men report that they sometimes change sexual partners, whereas most women report that they rarely change sexual partners.

Only 12% of men reported that they never substitute or switch sexual partners during a fantasy compared to 43% of women. Men also reported imagining sexual encounters with more than 1,000 partners in their lifetime four times as much as women did (32% versus 8%) Men are also more than four times as likely as women to have fantasies about group sex (Wilson, 1997). And 78% of men versus 32% of women answered "yes" to the question, "Would you ever engage in a threesome sexual situation?" (Hughes, Harrison, and Gallup, 2004).

Women's sexual fantasies, in contrast, often contain familiar partners. Of those surveyed, 59% of American women but only 28 % of American men reported that their sexual fantasies typically focus on someone with whom they were already romantically and sexually involved. Emotions and personality are crucial for women. Furthermore, 41% of the women but only 16% of the men report that they focus most heavily on the personal and emotional characteristics of the fantasized partner. Women are also more likely than men to emphasize romance and tenderness, as well as personal involvement in their sexual fantasies.

Studies of sex drive also reveal on-average sex differences. The largest study, involving more than 200,000 individuals from 53 nations, measured sex drive with these statements: "I have a strong sex drive" and "It doesn't take me much to get sexually excited" (Lippa, 2009). In every nation, from Croatia to Trinidad, men reported having a higher sex drive than did women. Similar findings also show up in masturbation rates and pornography consumption, both of which also show large sex differences (Petersen and Hyde, 2010). The sex difference in sex drive proved just as large in nations with high levels of gender equality such as Denmark and Sweden as it did in nations with lower levels of gender equality, such as Saudi Arabia and Turkey.

Sexual Exploitability

Goetz and her colleagues hypothesized that men oriented toward short-term mating should be especially sensitive to detecting and finding sexually attractive women who give off cues to being vulnerable to being sexually seduced or deceived (Goetz, Easton, Lewis, and Buss, 2012). They had photos of 36 women rated for different cues, and a separate group of men evaluated those photos for attractiveness as a short-term mate and as a long-term mate. Cues to sexual exploitability included being young, flirtatious, intoxicated, reckless, seeming immature, showing an open body posture, sleepy and wearing skimpy clothing.

Men found women displaying these cues to be sexually attractive for short-term mateship, but unattractive in the context of a long-term mate. These findings point to one possible evolved solution to the problem of detecting which women are sexually accessible, finding attractive women who display cues to sexual exploitability. Sexual exploitation, of course, is highly unethical, and a deeper understanding of men's sexual psychology around these issues can potentially lead to a reduction of this form of conduct.

Sexual Regret

Regret, the feeling of sorrow about something in the past, is hypothesised to function to improve future decision making by motivating people to avoid prior mistakes (Poore, Haselton, von Hippel, and Buss, 2005). Sexual regret could operate over two classes of actions: sexual actions taken (sexual commission) and missed sexual opportunities (sexual omission). Two independent groups of researchers have documented men, more than women, regret missed sexual opportunities (Roese et al., 2006; Galperin et al., 2013).

One study presented men and women with descriptions of regret such as "Should have tried harder to sleep with," "Kicked myself for missing out on a chance to have sex with" (Roese et al., 2006). Women were more likely to have regretted acts of sexual commission wishing that they had not had sex with someone that they did have sex with (Galperin et al., 2013). Men, on the other hand, regretted acts of sexual omission significantly more than did women.

Studies of actual hooking up revealed similar sex differences, with women more likely to experience negative emotions afterwards, whereas men experienced regret when the women they hooked up with wanted a more serious relationship (Lambert, Kahn, and Apple, 2003). Sexual regret, in short, has the hallmarks of an evolved feature in men designed to facilitate acting on future sexual opportunities and avoid entangling commitments.

The Attraction-Reduction Effect

One possible adaptation in men to facilitate the success of a short-term mating strategy is an attraction-reduction right after sexual intercourse (Haselton and Buss, 2001).

Men with more sex partners (indicating a short-term mating strategy) experienced a sharp decline in how sexually attractive they found their partner immediately following intercourse, whereas neither women nor men with less sexual experience showed this decline. The work on the attraction-reduction effect supports the hypothesis that men have sophisticated psychological adaptations designed to promote the success of a casual sexual strategy, one that motivates either a hasty post-copulatory departure to minimise investment in any one woman or a roving eye within the context of existing long-term mateship.

The Closing-Time Phenomenon

Do people experience changes in how attractive they perceive members of the opposite sex to be during an evening at singles bars? In one study, 137 men and 80 women in a bar were approached at 9:00 P.M., 10:30 P.M., and 12:00 A.M. and asked to rate the attractiveness of members of the opposite sex in the bar using a 10-point scale (Gladue and Delaney, 1990).

As closing time approached, men viewed women as increasingly attractive. The average judgment at 9:00 P.M.

was 5.5, but by midnight, it had increased to more than 6.5. Women's judgments of men's attractiveness also increased over time, but women perceived the male bar patrons as less attractive overall compared with the men's perceptions of the women. Women rated the men at the bar as just below the average of 5.0 at 9:00 P.M., increasing near the midnight closing time to only 5.5.

Men's shift in perceptions of attractiveness near closing time occurs regardless of how much alcohol they have consumed. Whether a man consumed a single drink, or six drinks had little effect on the shift in viewing women as more attractive. The often-noted "beer goggles" phenomenon, whereby women are presumed to be viewed as more attractive with men's increasing intoxication, may instead be attributable to a psychological mechanism that is sensitive to decreasing opportunities throughout the evening for casual sex.

As the evening progresses and a man has not yet been successful in picking up a woman, he views the remaining women in the bar as increasingly attractive, a shift that presumably increases his attempts to seek sex from those women.

The closing time phenomenon may represent a psychological solution to the problem of sexual accessibility: a context-specific lowering of standards as the likelihood of sexual opportunities starts to drop. The ancestral conditions that may have been selected for the closing time phenomenon are not clear since singles bars did not exist then. One speculation is that ancestral feasts or celebrations might have provided opportunities for short-term mating, ancestral analogues of modern-day singles bars.

The Lowering of Standards in Short-Term Mating

One psychological solution to securing a variety of casual sex partners is a relaxation of standards imposed by men for acceptable partners. High standards for attributes such as age, intelligence, marital status and personality function exclude most potential mates from consideration. However, relaxed standards ensure more numerous potential sex partners.

When college students provided information about the minimum and maximum acceptable ages of a partner for temporary and permanent sexual relationships (Buss and Schmitt, 1993), college men accepted an age range roughly four years wider than do women for a sexual hook-up. Men at this age are willing to mate in the short run with members of the opposite sex who are as young as 16 and as old as 28, whereas women prefer men who are at least 18 but no older than 26. This relaxation of age restrictions by men does not apply to committed mating.

Men also express significantly lower standards than the women on 41 of the 67 characteristics named as potentially desirable in a casual mate. For brief encounters, men require a lower level of assets such as athletic, charming, cooperative, educated, emotionally stable, generous, honest, independent, intellectual, kind, loyal, responsible, sense of humour, sociable, spontaneous and wealth. Men's relaxation of standards across a range of attributes helps to solve the problem of gaining access to a variety of sex partners.

The Problem of Identifying Fertile Women

A clear evolutionary prediction is that men seeking short-term mates would prefer women who displayed cues correlated with fertility. A maximally fertile woman would have the highest probability of getting pregnant from a single act of sex. In contrast, men seeking long-term mates might be predicted to prefer younger women of higher reproductive value, because such women will be more likely to reproduce in the future.

This distinction of fertility versus reproductive value does not guarantee that selection will have fashioned two different standards of attraction in men, one for casual sex and another for a marriage partner. The key point is that this distinction can be used to generate a hypothesis about shifts in age preferences, which we can then test.

The Problem of Partner Number or Variety

Successful pursuit of short-term mating requires an adaptation that is motivational, something that would impel men toward a variety of sex partners.

One solution is the desire for sex with a variety of different women (Symons, 1979). A second specialised adaptation is a relaxation of standards for an acceptable short-term partner. Another predicted adaptation is to impose minimum time constraints to let little time elapse before seeking sexual intercourse.

The Problem of Sexual Accessibility

Advantages would accrue to men who focused their mating efforts on women who were sexually accessible. Courtship, energy, and temporal resources devoted to women who are unlikely to consent to sex would interfere with the successful pursuit of short-term mating. Specialised adaptations for solving the problem of sexual accessibility might occur in the form of men's short-term mate preferences.

Men might disfavour women who show signs of being conservative, having a low sex drive and are prudish since these qualities might suggest lower odds of successful short-term mating. Behaviour and clothing that signal potential sexual availability might be desired by men in short-term mates too.

Time Elapsed Before Seeking Intercourse

Another solution to the problem of gaining sexual access to a variety of partners is to let little time elapse between meeting a desired potential partner and seeking sexual intercourse. College men and women rated how likely they would be to consent to sex with someone they viewed as desirable if they had known the person for only an hour, a day, a week, a month, 6 months, a year, 2 years, or 5 years (Buss and Schmitt, 1993). Both men and women say that they would probably have sex after knowing a desirable potential mate for 5 years. However, at every shorter interval, men exceeded women in the reported likelihood of having sex.

As with their desires, men's inclination to let little time elapse before seeking sexual intercourse offers a partial solution to the adaptive problem of gaining sexual access to a variety of partners. Men's greater likelihood of consenting to sexual intercourse after little time has elapsed has now been extensively replicated in samples of varying ages and geographical locations within both the United States (Schmitt, Shackelford, and Buss, 2001) and Norway (Kennair et al., 2009).

Conflicts Between the Sexes

Anti-Rape Adaptations

Although the controversy over explanations of rape has centred on the motivations of men, it is critical to examine rape victims. There is one point about victim psychology that all theoretical camps agree on: rape is abhorrent and often inflicts heavy costs on the victim. We do not need a formal theory for this insight, but it is important to examine why rape is experienced as extremely traumatic by victims.

From an evolutionary perspective, the costs of rape begin with the interference with women's mate choice, an essential part of women's sexual strategies. A raped woman risks an unwanted and untimely pregnancy with a man she has not chosen. Furthermore, victims of rape risk being blamed or punished, resulting in damage to their reputations and their future desirability on the mating market. If they are already mated, they risk being abandoned by their regular mates. Raped women often suffer psychologically: anxiety, depression, fear, humiliation, and rage are common in the aftermath.

Given all these large costs, if rape has occurred throughout human evolutionary history, it would be astonishing if selection had not favoured in women the evolution of defences to prevent becoming a victim. Note that this is a separate issue from that of whether men have evolved adaptations to rape. In principle, women could have evolved anti-rape defences even if rape has been entirely a non-adaptive by-product in men. Although we cannot go back in time to determine with absolute certainty, historical records and anthropological ethnographies suggest strongly that rape has occurred across cultures and over time (Buss, 2003; Lalumiere et al., 2005). Indeed, the Amazonian groups studied by Thomas Gregor have specific words for both rape (antapai) and gang rape (aintyawakakinapai) (Gregor, 1985). Evolutionary anthropologist Smuts summarises this evidence: "Although the prevalence of male violence against women varies from place to place, cross-cultural surveys indicate that societies in which men rarely attack or rape women are the exception, not the norm" (Smuts, 1992).

If then rape has been a recurrent hazard for women, what defences might have evolved to lower the odds of becoming a victim? Several have been hypothesized: the formation of alliances with other males as "special friends" for protection (Smuts, 1992); the cultivation of female-female coalitions for protection (Smuts 1992); mate selection based on qualities of men such as physical size and social dominance that deter other men from sexual aggression (Wilson and Mesnick, 1997); the development of specialised fears that motivate women to avoid situations in which they might be in danger of rape (Chavanne and Gallup, 1998); the avoidance of risky activities during ovulation to decrease the odds of sexual assault when they are most likely to conceive (Chavanne and Gallup, 1998); psychological pain from rape that motivates women to avoid rape in the future (Thornhill and Palmer, 2000) and a threat management system that motivates women to avoid out-of-group males, on the assumption that intergroup conflict would have put women in danger of sexual coercion from outgroup men.

Although research into these hypothesized defences has barely begun, it shows promise. Women who are not taking oral contraceptives tend to avoid risky activities, such as going to a bar alone or walking in a dimly lit area, more when they are ovulating than at other times in the cycle (Chavanne and Gallup, 1998; Bröder and Hohmann, 2003). Greater fear of rape among women who perceived themselves as vulnerable to sexual coercion increases behavioural precautions, such as avoiding being alone with men they do not know well, avoiding out-group men, and avoiding men who come on strong sexually (McDonald, Donnellan, Cesario, and Navarrete, 2015). Young women experience more fear of rape than do older women, who are more likely to fear being robbed or burgled, suggesting that fear might be tracking the risks of rape (Pawson and Banks, 1993). A study in 2013 of 844 women in Slovakia, for example, found that virgin women tend to engage in more rape avoidance than nonvirgin women (Prokop, 2013) and although direct tests of the bodyguard-centred hypothesises have not yet been conducted, married women report lower rates of rape than do single women (Wilson and Mesnick, 1997).

McKibbin, Shackelford, Goetz, Bates, and Starrett (2009) have discovered four common strategies women use to avoid rape: (i) avoiding strange or dangerous men (e.g., avoiding men with a reputation of forcing themselves on women); (ii) avoiding appearing sexually receptive (e.g., not wearing revealing clothing); (iii) avoiding being alone (e.g., staying close to others when going out), and (iv) being prepared and showing awareness of surroundings (e.g., looking around before exiting the car). Women who rate themselves high on physical attractiveness are significantly more likely to avoid being alone and show heightened preparedness and awareness of their surroundings (McKibbin et al., 2010). Another predictor was relationship status: women in committed long-term relationships also avoided being alone and were more likely than single women to avoid appearing sexually receptive.

In summary, the modest empirical work so far suggests much promise for uncovering women's anti-rape defences. Given the alarming rates of rape in modern environments, research is urgently needed on women's anti-rape strategies and their relative effectiveness, whether or not such strategies ultimately turn out to be specialized evolved adaptations or by-products of more general cognitive and emotional mechanisms.

Cognitive Biases in Sexual Mind Reading

Humans live in an uncertain mating world. We must make inferences about others' intentions and emotional states: does that smile signal sexual interest or mere friendliness? How attracted is he to her? How committed is she to him? Some psychological states, such as smouldering passions for other people, are intentionally concealed, rendering uncertainty greater and inferences more tortuous. We are forced to make inferences about intentions and concealed deeds using an array of cues that are only probabilistically related to the deeds' occurrence. An unexplained scent on one's romantic partner, for example, could signal sexual betrayal or an innocuous aroma acquired from a casual conversation.

In "reading the minds of others," there are two ways to go wrong: (i) you can infer a psychological state that is not there, such as assuming sexual interest when it is absent or (ii) you can fail to infer a psychological state that is there, such as remaining oblivious to another's true romantic yearnings. According to error management theory, it would be exceedingly unlikely that the cost-benefit consequences of the two types of errors would be identical across their many occurrences (Haselton, 2003; Haselton and Buss, 2000, 2003; Haselton and Nettle, 2006). We intuitively understand this in the context of smoke alarms, which are typically set to be hypersensitive to any hint of smoke. The costs of occasional false alarms are minor compared to the catastrophic costs of failing to detect a real house fire. Error management theory extends this logic to cost-benefit consequences in evolutionary fitness.

Accordingly, if error management theory is correct, asymmetries in the cost-benefit consequences of mind-reading inferences, if they recur over evolutionary time, create selection pressures that produce predictable cognitive biases. Just as smoke alarms are "biased" to produce more false positives than false negatives, error management theory predicts that evolved mind-reading mechanisms will be biased to produce more of one type of inferential error than another. Two mind-reading biases have been explored in mating. The first is the sexual overperception bias, whereby men possess mind-reading biases designed to minimise the costs of missed sexual opportunities. Men appear to falsely infer that a woman is sexually interested in them when she happens to stop at the local bar for a drink, merely smiles or perchance touches his arm. Interestingly, men who view themselves as especially high in mate value are especially prone to experiencing the sexual overperception bias (Haselton, 2003). Men who are dispositioned to pursue a short-term mating strategy also exhibit a more pronounced sexual overperception bias - a bias that would facilitate the success of a short-term mating strategy by minimising lost opportunities (Lenton, Bryan, Hastie, and Fischer, 2007; Perilloux et al., 2012; Kohl and Robertson, 2014).

The second is the commitment scepticism bias in women (Haselton and Buss, 2000). According to this hypothesis, women have evolved an inferential bias designed to underestimate men's actual level of romantic commitment to them early in the courtship. This bias functions to minimise the costs of being sexually deceived by men who feign commitment to pursue a strategy of casual sex. If men give flowers or gifts to women, for example, the recipients tend to underestimate the extent to which these offerings signal commitment in comparison with "objective" outside observers. Of course, there are good reasons for women's commitment scepticism. Men who are motivated to seek casual sex frequently attempt to deceive women about their commitment, social status, and even fondness for children (Haselton et al., 2005) - domains of deception about which women are well aware (Keenan, Gallup, Goulet, and Kulkarni, 1997). Women's commitment scepticism bias can be reduced or eliminated when men display strong behavioural cues to commitment, although women nonetheless need more behavioural evidence than do men to infer that their partner is truly committed to them (Brown and Olkhov, 2015).

Younger women in particular have more to lose by being deceived about a man's commitment. Older post-menopausal women not only have less to lose by such deception but have been hypothesized not to display the commitment scepticism bias, since they might miss out on opportunities to partner with men who could help them raise their children and grandchildren (Cyrus, Schwarz, and Hassebrauck, 2011). One study conducted in Germany replicated the commitment scepticism bias in young women but found that this bias was absent in a sample of women in their 50s (Cyrus et al., 2011).

Error management theory, therefore, offers a fresh perspective on human mating problems, suggesting that some errors reflect functional adaptations rather than actual flaws in the psychological machinery. It provides new insights into why men and women get into certain types of conflict: for example, men's sexual overperception bias leads to unwanted sexual come-ons or sexual harassment. Knowledge of these biases and the evolutionary logic by which they came about might help men and women to read each other's mating minds more accurately and, ideally, reduce some forms of sexual conflict.

Commitment Deception

Another manifestation of conflict over sexual access comes from research on deception between the sexes. Men report intentionally deceiving women about emotional commitment. When 112 college men were asked whether they had ever exaggerated the depth of their feelings for a woman to have sex with her, 71% admitted to having done so, compared with only 39% of the women (Buss, 1994b; Haselton et al., 2005). In a study in which women reported on their actual experiences of deception at the hands of men, they reported the following forms of deception (percentage of women reporting them is in parentheses): "falsely implied that he had stronger feelings for me than he really had" (44%); "exaggerated how sincere, trustworthy, or kind he was" (42%); "led me to believe that we were more compatible than we really were" (36%); "led me to believe that he had stronger feelings for me to have sex with me" (25%) (Haselton et al., 2005). Men high on Dark Triad traits (narcissism, Machiavellianism, and psychopathy) are more prone to using these forms of deceptive tactics (Jonason, Lyons, Baughman, and Vernon, 2014).

In human courtship, women shoulder the costs of being deceived about a potential mate's resources and commitment more heavily. An ancestral man who made a poor choice of a sex partner risked losing only a small portion of his time, energy, and resources, although he might also have evoked the rage of a jealous husband or a protective father. An ancestral woman who made a poor choice of a casual mate, allowing herself to be deceived about the man's long-term intentions or willingness to devote resources to her, however, risked untimely pregnancy and unaided childrearing.

Because the deceived can suffer severe losses, there must have been tremendous selection pressure for the evolution of psychological vigilance to detect cues to deception and to prevent its occurrence. The modern generation is merely experiencing another cycle in the endless spiral of an evolutionary arms race between deception perpetrated by individuals of one sex and detection accomplished by individuals of the other. As the deceptive tactics grow more subtle and refined, the co-evolved ability to penetrate deception becomes more acute.

Women have evolved strategies to guard against deception. When a woman seeks a committed relationship, the first line of defence is imposing courtship costs by requiring time, energy, and commitment before consenting to sex. More time permits more assessment. It allows a woman greater opportunity to evaluate a man, to assess how committed he is to her, and to detect whether he is burdened by prior commitments to other women and children.

Evolved Rape Adaptations

Rape may be defined as the use of force or the threat of force to obtain sexual intercourse. One of the most controversial issues in evolutionary psychology is whether men have evolved specialised adaptations to rape under certain circumstances or whether rape is a non-adaptive by-product of other evolved mechanisms. Among scorpionflies, there is evidence that males have a special anatomical clamp that functions solely in the context of raping a female (Thornhill, 1980). It is not used in other mating contexts, during which the male presents a nuptial gift as an inducement for the female to copulate. There is also evidence for specialized rape strategy in orangutans, although this might be the exception among primates since bonobos and common chimpanzees appear to lack a distinctive rape strategy (Maggioncalda and Sapolsky, 2002).

The rape-as-adaptation theory proposes that selection has favoured ancestral males who raped in certain circumstances. Proponents of this theory advance the hypothesis that at least six specialized adaptations might have evolved in the male mind (Thornhill and Palmer, 2000): assessment of the vulnerability of potential rape victims (e.g., during warfare or in non-warfare contexts in which a woman lacks the protection of husband or kin); a context-sensitive "switch" that motivates rape in men who lack sexual access to consenting partners (e.g., "loser" males who cannot obtain mates through regular channels of courtship); a preference for fertile rape victims; an increase in sperm counts of rape ejaculates compared with those occurring in consensual sex; sexual arousal to the use of force or to female resistance to consensual sex and marital rape in circumstances in which sperm competition might exist (e.g., when there is evidence or suspicion of female infidelity).

In contrast, the non-adaptive by-product theory proposes that rape is a non-designed and non-selected-for by-product of other evolved mechanisms, such as the male desire for sexual variety, a desire for sex without investment, a psychological sensitivity to sexual opportunities, and the general capacity to use physical aggression to achieve a variety of goals (Symons, 1979).

Unfortunately, clear-cut evidence bearing on these competing theories is lacking. Rape is a common occurrence during the war, but theft, looting, property damage, and cruelty to the defeated are also common. Are there specialized adaptations for each of these behaviours, or are they by-products of other mechanisms? Definitive studies have not been conducted.

Rapists tend to target young, reproductive-aged women disproportionately. Indeed, roughly 70% of rape victims fall between the ages of 16 and 35 (Thornhill and Thornhill, 1983). Another study of sexual assaults during robberies found that male robbers of all ages were most likely to rape women in the 15- to 29-year age range (Felson and Cundiff, 2012). The fact that rapists tend to victimize young, fertile women, however, is not definitive evidence for or against the competing theories of rape. This result could be due to men's evolved preference for cues to fertile women in regular mating contexts, and hence rape-specific adaptations are not needed to explain this finding.

Income and Status Striving

Women's mate-retention tactics, in contrast to those of men, were not hypothesised to be a function of the husband's age or physical attractiveness, and indeed they were not. Women's efforts at mate retention, however, were hypothesised to be linked with the value of their mates on the dimensions of income and status striving - the degree to which the husband devotes his efforts to getting ahead in the status and work hierarchy (Buss and Shackelford, 1997c). These are sex-linked components of mate value that women across cultures desire in long-term mates.

To test this hypothesis, Buss and Shackelford in 1997 correlated mate- retention tactics with the partner's income and with four measures of status striving. These measures include the degree to which a person uses deception or manipulation to get ahead, industriousness and hard work, social networking, and ingratiating oneself with superiors. Women married to men with higher incomes reported greater appearance enhancement, possessive ornamentation, self-abasement, submission, vigilance, and violence toward a partner.

Women married to men who devoted more effort to status striving reported significantly more appearance enhancement, emotional manipulation, possessive ornamentation, resource display and verbal signals of possession than women married to men who were low on status striving. These correlations remained significant even after statistically controlling for other factors, such as the ages of the spouses and the length of their relationship.

Individuals within each sex also differ in their mate-retention tactics. Taller men, indicating higher mate value, perform fewer mate-retention tactics (Brewer and Riley, 2009). Men high in mate value (e.g., as gauged by high economic prospects) also perform more benefit-bestowing mate-retention tactics (Miner, Shackelford, and Starratt, 2009; Miner, Starratt, and Shackelford, 2009). Men lower in mate value use more cost-inflicting mate-retention tactics (e.g., insulting their partners to lower their self-esteem), perhaps because they lack the resources to bestow benefits. Those high on the Dark Triad of personality traits (narcissism, Machiavellianism, and psychopathy) tend to use aggressive cost-inflicting mate-retention tactics (Jonason, Li, and Buss, 2010). Both men and women who score low on the honesty–humility personality trait tend to use more manipulative, deceptive, and exploitative mate-retention tactics (Holden, Zeigler-Hill, Pham, and Shackelford, 2014).

Jealousy

Mates gained must be retained to fulfil the reproductive potential inherent in the initial mate selection. Threats to mate retention come from several sources. The first of these is the presence of mate poachers, rivals who attempt to lure someone else's mate away either for a sexual encounter or for a long-term relationship (Schmitt and Buss, 2001). Mate poaching has been documented to be a widespread mating strategy across cultures (Schmitt et al., 2004). The second often related threat comes from a mate's infidelity, which could be in the form of short-term sexual infidelity or a longer-term departure from the relationship. Because both threats have been recurrent adaptive problems, selection has favoured the evolution of defences to fend off mate poachers, to deter a mate's sexual infidelity, and to retain a mate for the long run. Evolutionary psychologists have hypothesised that the emotion of jealousy and behavioural tactics of mate retention have evolved to deal with these adaptive problems, problems that differ in certain respects for men and women (Symons, 1979; Daly et al., 1982; Buss, 2013).

The adaptive problem of cuckoldry is magnified in men because of the tremendous investment they often channel toward their children. If a man is cuckolded, he risks investing all of his resources in a rival man's child. Not only does he lose his investment, but he also stands to lose the investment of his partner, who would now be investing her efforts in another man's child. Ancestral men who failed to solve this adaptive problem not only risked suffering direct reproductive losses but also risked losing status and reputation, which could have seriously impaired their ability to attract other mates.

Jealousy might help to solve this adaptive problem in several ways. First, it might sensitize a man to circumstances in which his partner might be unfaithful, promoting vigilance. Second, it might prompt actions designed to curtail his partner's contact with other men. Third, it might cause him to increase his efforts to fulfil his partner's desires so that she would have less incentive to stray. And fourth, jealousy might prompt a man to threaten or otherwise fend off rivals who show sexual interest in his partner. One clear evolutionary prediction is that a man's jealousy should focus heavily on the potential sexual contact that his partner might have with another man since such sexual contact jeopardizes his paternity of offspring.

Women also face a profound adaptive problem because of a partner's infidelity, but it is not defined by a compromise in a woman's certainty that she is the mother of her children. Rather, because men tend to channel investments and resources to women with whom they have sex, a husband might devote time, attention, energy, and resources to another woman and her children rather than to his wife and children. For these reasons, evolutionary psychologists have predicted that women's jealousy would be more likely to focus on cues to the long-term diversion of a man's commitments, such as his becoming emotionally involved with another woman (Buss, Larsen, Westen, and Semmelroth, 1992).

Mate Deprivation Hypothesis

According to the mate deprivation hypothesis, men who have experienced deprivation of sexual access to women will be more likely to use sexually aggressive tactics (Thornhill and Thornhill, 1983, 1992; Quinsey and

Lalumiere, 1995; Lalumiere, Chalmers, Quinsey, and Seto, 1996). Perhaps men have evolved a conditional mating strategy, when they cannot secure mates through the usual means of attraction and courtship, they experience deprivation, which prompts them to use sexually aggressive tactics to avoid being excluded entirely.

This hypothesis was tested on a sample of 156 heterosexual males with a mean age of 20 (Lalumiere et al., 1996). The measures of sexual coercion included both nonphysical (e.g., "Have you ever had sexual intercourse with a woman even though she didn't want to because she felt pressured by your continual arguments?") and physical coercion (e.g., "Have you ever had sexual intercourse with a woman when she didn't want to because you used some degree of physical force?"). The measure of mating success was assessed by the self-perceived mating success scale, which included items such as "Members of the opposite sex that I like tend to like me back"; "I receive many compliments from members of the opposite sex"; "I receive sexual invitations from members of the opposite sex"; and "Members of the opposite sex are attracted to me."

The results contradicted the predictions the authors derived from the mate deprivation hypothesis of sexual aggression: men who scored high on self-perceived mating success also tended to score high on the measures of sexual aggression. Furthermore, men who evaluated their future earning potential as high tended to use more physical coercion than did men who perceived their future earning potential is low. Another study found a positive but not significant correlation between sexual coercive tactics and mating success (Camilleri, Quinsey, and Tapscott, 2009). And a third study found that men who commit sexual assault report a higher number of lifetime sex partners (Ellis, Widmayer, and Palmer, 2009). In summary, the results fail to support the mate deprivation hypothesis.

Occurrence and Timing of Sex

Disagreements about the occurrence and timing of sex might be the most common sources of conflict between men and women. In a study of 121 college students who kept daily diaries of their dating activities for 4 weeks, 47% reported one or more disagreements about their desired level of sexual intimacy (Byers and Lewis, 1988). These disagreements show a predictable sex difference. In one study of Australian undergraduate students, for example, 53% of the women in the study reported that at least one man had "overestimated the level of sexual intimacy... desired," whereas 45% of the men reported that at least one woman had "underestimated the level of sexual intimacy... desired" (Paton and Mannison, 1995).

Men sometimes seek sex with a minimum of investment. Men often guard their resources and are extraordinarily choosy about who they invest those resources in. They often preserve their investment and resources for long-term mates. Because women often pursue a long-term sexual strategy, they often seek to obtain investment, or signals of investment, before consenting to sex. Yet the investment that women seek is precisely the investment that men most vigorously guard. The sex that men seek is precisely the resource that women are so selective about allocating.

Ovulation Status

A man's risk of being genetically cuckolded falls most heavily when his partner is ovulating. Consequently, evolutionary psychologists predicted that men would increase their mate-retention efforts at precisely this time in their partner's menstrual cycle. Several studies, using women's reports of their partner's mate-retention efforts, have shown this effect (Gangestad et al., 2005; Haselton and Gangestad, 2006; Pillsworth and Haselton, 2006). Furthermore, women who are mated to men low on good genes indicators, such as sexual attractiveness, had partners who were especially keen on mate-retention efforts when the women were ovulating, showering them with more love and attention at this time. These findings reveal a fundamental conflict between the sexes: men mate guard their partners most vigorously at precisely the time when the man is at the greatest risk of genetic cuckoldry.

Partner Rapists

An estimated 10% to 26% of married women experience rape from their husbands (McKibbin, Shackelford, Goetz, and Starratt, 2008). According to one hypothesis, this form of rape represents an adaptation to sperm competition: men whose wives have been sexually unfaithful or who suspect their wives of infidelity force sex to combat the sperm from competing males (Goetz and Shackelford, 2009). Two empirical studies confirmed that men who knew or suspected their partners of infidelity indeed were more likely to use a variety of sexually coercive tactics, including physical force (Goetz and Shackelford, 2009). Another study also found that direct cues to a partner's infidelity were linked with a higher proclivity to use sexual coercion (Camilleri and Quinsey, 2009a).

Not all men who perceive that their partners are unfaithful, however, resort to sexual coercion. One study found that partner rapists tended to score high on psychopathy, supporting the life-history strategy theory of individual differences in rape proclivity (Camilleri and Quinsey, 2009b; Figueredo et al., 2010). Another study found that only men who perceive themselves to be equal or higher in mate value than their partner and perceive partner infidelity resort to sexually coercive tactics (Starratt, Popp, and Shackelford, 2008). In contrast, among men who perceive themselves to be lower in mate value, there is no link between perceptions of partner infidelity and the use of sexually coercive tactics. Simply put, although the sperm competition hypothesis of partner rape receives some empirical support, it must be qualified by individual differences in life-history strategy (psychopathy) and relative mate value.

Today there is good evidence for individual differences among men in rape proclivity. Psychopaths, for example, who tend to pursue an exploitative life-history strategy, seem especially prone to use sexual coercion, both with non-partners and with partners whom they suspect might be sexually unfaithful.

Resource Access

The generalisation that men tend to wield power and control resources should not obscure the fact that in nearly every culture, women contribute substantially to the accrual of economic resources. In hunter-gatherer societies, for example, women sometimes contribute 60% to 80% of the calories through gathering food from plants (Tooby and DeVore, 1987). Furthermore, women often exert considerable power through various means, including exerting preferential mate choice, divorcing men under certain conditions, controlling or regulating men's access to their sexuality, and influencing their sons, lovers, fathers, husbands, sisters, mothers, and grandchildren (Buss, 2016 b).

It cannot be disputed that men often use resources to control or influence women. If men possess the resources that women want or need, then men can use those resources to control women. In the mating domain, men use their resources to attract women. Furthermore, once in relationships, women who lack resources often feel at the mercy of their partners for fear of losing those resources (Wilson and Daly, 1992). These key points, men's control of resources and men's use of resources to control women, appear to be issues of agreement between evolutionary psychologists and feminist scholars (Buss, 1996a).

Feminist scholars often trace the roots of women's oppression by men to patriarchy, a term referring to men's dominance over women in the family specifically and in society more generally (Smuts, 1995). A reasonable scientific question pertains to the origins of the phenomena that are subsumed under this term.

Sexual Aggressiveness

Sexual aggressiveness is one strategy men use to minimize their investment for sexual access, although this strategy carries costs in the form of retaliation and damage to reputation. Acts of sexual aggression are exemplified by the man's demanding or forcing sexual intimacy, failing to get mutual agreement for sex, and touching a woman's body without her permission. In one study, college women were asked to evaluate 147 potentially upsetting actions that men could do to them on a scale ranging from 1 (not at all upsetting) to 7 (extremely upsetting) (Buss, 1989b). Women rated acts of sexual aggression on average to be 6.5. No other kinds of acts that men could perform, including verbal abuse and non-sexual physical abuse, were judged by women to be as upsetting as sexual aggression, a finding independently verified in a study of Dutch individuals (ter Laak, Olthof, and Aleva, 2003).

Men, in sharp contrast, seem less bothered when a woman is sexually aggressive; they see it as relatively innocuous compared with other sources of distress. On the same seven-point scale, for example, men judged the group of sexually aggressive acts to be 3.02, or only slightly upsetting when performed by a woman. Other sources of distress, such as a mate's infidelity and verbal or physical abuse, were far more upsetting to the men, 6.04 and 5.55, respectively, than sexual aggression by a woman.

Sexual Harassment

Disagreements over sexual access occur not just in the context of dating and marital relationships but also in the workplace, where people sometimes seek casual and long-term mates. Sexual harassment is defined as "unwanted and unsolicited sexual attention from other individuals in the workplace" (Terpstra and Cook, 1985). Sexual harassment can range from mild forms, such as unwanted staring and sexual comments, to physical violations, such as the unwanted touching of breasts, buttocks, or crotch. Sexual harassment produces obvious conflict between the sexes and is the result of differences between men's and women's evolved psychologies (Browne, 2002, 2010).

Sexual harassment is typically motivated by the possibility that a come-on might lead to a short-term sexual encounter, although this does not exclude the possibility that it is sometimes motivated by the desire to exercise power or to seek lasting romantic relationships. The view that sexual harassment is a product of the evolved sexual strategies of men and women is supported by the profiles of typical victims, including elements such as age, gender, marital status, people's reactions to unwanted sexual advances, physical attractiveness and the conditions under which harassment occurs.

One study of 1,199 Norwegian high school students discovered that men who are dispositioned to pursue a short-term mating strategy are much more likely to perpetrate sexual harassment (Kennair and Bendixen, 2012). Indeed, unwanted sexual solicitations are better predicted by a short-term mating strategy than any other predictor in a subsequent Norwegian study, more predictive than porn consumption and measures of sexist attitudes (Bendixen and Kennair, 2017). Importantly, men high on the Dark Triad personality traits (narcissism, Machiavellianism, and psychopathy) tend to pursue a short-term mating strategy and are especially likely to engage in sexual harassment (Zeigler-Hill, Besser, Morag, and Campbell, 2016).

Victims of sexual harassment are typically women. In one study of complaints filed with the Illinois Department of Human Rights over two years, women filed 76 complaints, whereas men filed only five. Another study of 10,644 federal government employees found that 42% of the women but only 15% of the men had experienced sexual harassment at some point (Gutek, 1985). Of the sexual harassment complaints filed in one Canadian province, 93 cases were filed by women and only two by men. Women are generally the victims of sexual harassment and men are generally the perpetrators. Nonetheless, given the tendency of women to experience greater distress concerning acts of sexual pushiness or aggressiveness, it is likely that women would be more upset than men by the same acts of sexual harassment (Colarelli et al., 2001; Buss, 2016 b).

Although any woman may be the target of sexual harassment, the victims are disproportionately concentrated among young, physically attractive, and single women. Women over age 43 are far less likely than younger women to experience sexual harassment (Studd and Gattiker, 1991). One study found that women between the ages of 20 and 35 filed 72% of the complaints of harassment, although they represented only 43% of the labour force at the time. Women over age 45, who represented 28% of the workforce, filed only 5% of the complaints. Moreover, women who tend to pursue a short-term mating strategy are more likely to become victims of sexual harassment (Kennair and Bendixen, 2012).

Reactions to sexual harassment follow the logic predicted by strategic interference theory. When men and women were asked how they would feel if a colleague of the opposite sex asked them to have sex, 63% of the women said they would be insulted, whereas a minority, 17% of the women, said they would feel flattered. Men's reactions were just the opposite: Only 15% said they would be insulted, whereas 67% said they would feel flattered. These results support strategic interference theory.

The degree of distress that women experience after sexual advances, however, depends in part on the status of the harasser. In one study, 109 college women rated how upset they would be if a man they did not know, whose occupational status varied from low to high, persisted in asking them out on a date despite their repeated refusals (Buss, 2016 b). On a seven-point scale, women would be most upset by persistent advances from construction workers (4.04), garbage collectors (4.32), cleaning men (4.19), and gas station attendants (4.13) and least upset by persistent advances by premedical students (2.65), graduate students (2.80), or successful rock stars (2.71). Status and power, however, interact: Women find acts of harassment most harassing from a low-status man who has power over them (Colarelli and Haaland, 2002).

It is important to note that sexual harassment in the workplace puts victims in terribly awkward and difficult situations. Victims often are forced to navigate rejecting unwanted advances without jeopardizing their careers or risking retaliation from the perpetrator. Perpetrators typically fail to realise the difficulties their behaviour inflicts on targets and men often underestimate how upsetting acts of sexual aggression are to women. These findings potentially have practical applications for educating men and women in workplace settings, ideally for reaching a better understanding of women's and men's minds and for reducing sexual harassment.

Sexual Intent

A major source of conflict is that men sometimes infer sexual interest on the part of a woman when it does not exist. This phenomenon has no doubt be observed countless times. In one study, 98 male and 102 female college students viewed a 10-minute videotape of a conversation in which a female student visits a male professor's office to ask for more time to complete a term paper.

The actors in the film were a female drama student and a professor in the theatre department. Neither the student nor the professor acted flirtatious or overtly sexual, although both were instructed to behave in a friendly manner. People who witnessed the tape then rated the likely intentions of the woman using a seven-point scale. Women watching the interaction were more likely to say that she was trying to be friendly, with an average rating of 6.45, and not sexy (2.00) or seductive (1.89). Men, also perceiving friendliness (6.09), were significantly more likely than women to infer seductive (3.38) and sexual intentions (3.84).

In a cross-cultural test of the sexual over-perception bias, a sample of 196 Brazilian college students, 98 men and 98 women evaluated four hypothetical scenarios presented in Portuguese (DeSouza, Pierce, Zanelli, and Hutz, 1992). A parallel sample of 204 American college students evaluated the scenarios in English. In each scenario, a man and a woman spent time together at a party. The scenarios differed in whether the participants had been drinking alcohol and in whether the woman agreed to go back to the man's dorm room with him.

Brazilian college students consistently perceived more sexuality in the characters' behaviour than did the American college students, with mean scores of 18.77 and

14.27, respectively. Gender differences were also highly significant. Men across both cultures perceived more sexual intent in the characters' actions than did women, with mean scores of 17.53 and 15.50, respectively. The male sexual over-perception bias has also been robustly replicated in Norway, one of the most sexually egalitarian countries in the world (Bendixen, 2014).

When in doubt, men infer sexual interest. Men act on their inferences, occasionally opening up sexual opportunities. If over evolutionary history even a tiny fraction of these inferences led to sex, men would have evolved lower thresholds for inferring women's sexual interest. This male mechanism is susceptible to manipulation. Women sometimes use their sexuality as one such tactic.

An interesting real-world demonstration of the sexual overperception bias occurred when a supermarket chain implemented a "superior customer service" program: store employees were instructed to smile at customers and make eye contact with them. The program backfired when several female employees filed sexual harassment charges against the supermarket. Their friendly actions caused some of the male customers to interpret their behaviour as signalling sexual interest, leading to sexual comments, overt sexual come-ons, and even stalking (Browne, 2006).

The fact that men are likely to perceive that women are interested in them sexually when they are not, combined with women's intentional exploitation of this psychological mechanism, creates a potentially volatile mix. The differing sexual strategies of men and women lead to conflicts over desired levels of sexual intimacy, over men's feelings that women lead them on, and over women's feelings that men are too pushy about having sex.

Sexual Withholding

Men consistently complain about women's sexual withholding, defined by such acts as being sexually teasing, saying no to intercourse, and leading a man on and then stopping him. Both sexes are bothered by sexual withholding, but men significantly more so than women.

For women, sexual withholding fulfils several possible functions. One is to preserve their ability to choose men of high quality who are willing to commit emotionally and invest materially. Women withhold sex from certain men and selectively allocate it to others. Moreover, by withholding sex, women increase their value. They render it a scarce resource. Scarcity increases the price that men are willing to pay for it. If the only way men can gain sexual access is by heavy investment, then they will make that investment. Under conditions of sexual scarcity, men who fail to invest fail to secure copulations. This creates another conflict between a man and a woman: her withholding interferes with his strategy of gaining sexual access sooner and with fewer emotional strings attached.

Another function of sexual withholding is to manipulate men's perception of a woman's value as a mate. Because highly desirable women are more sexually inaccessible to the average man by definition, women sometimes exploit men's perceptions of their desirability by withholding sexual access. A final possible function of sexual withholding, at least initially, is to encourage a man to evaluate a woman as a long-term rather than a short-term mate. Granting sexual access early can cause men to view a woman as a casual sex partner. They may perceive her as too promiscuous and too sexually available, characteristics that men avoid in committed mates.

Strategic Interference

Human conflict is a universal feature of social interaction, and it occurs in many forms. Evolutionary psychologists have predicted conflict between the sexes, but not because men and women compete for the same reproductive resources. Rather, many sources of conflict between the sexes can be traced to evolved differences in sexual strategies. Both sexes have evolved short-term and long-term mating strategies, but the nature of these strategies differs for the sexes. One of the most important differences pertains to short-term mating strategies. Men, far more than women, have evolved a stronger desire for sexual variety. This desire manifests itself in many forms, including seeking sexual access sooner, more persistently, and more aggressively than women typically desire. Conversely, women have evolved to be more discriminating in short-term mating, typically delaying sexual intercourse beyond what men usually desire. The sexes cannot simultaneously fulfil these conflicting sexual desires. This is an example of a phenomenon called strategic interference.

Strategic interference occurs when a person employs a particular strategy to achieve a goal and another person blocks the successful enactment of that strategy. If a woman delays sexual intercourse until she feels some emotional involvement or commitment from a man, for example, and the man persists in his sexual advances even after the woman has indicated her desire to wait, then the result is interference with the woman's sexual strategy. At the same time, however, the delays imposed by the woman interfere with the man's short-term mating strategy of seeking sex sooner. In sum, men and women come into conflict not because they are competing for the same resources, as often occurs in same-sex strategic interference, but rather because the strategy of an individual of one sex can interfere with the strategy of an individual of the other.

The theory of strategic interference applies not just to conflicts about the timing of sex. Conflict can pervade all relations between the sexes, from contact in the workplace and on the dating scene to skirmishes that occur during a marriage. Sexual harassment is a form of strategic interference in the workplace. Deception on the dating scene is another form of strategic interference. A man who deceives a woman about his marital status and a woman who deceives a man about her age both violate the desires of the opposite sex, forms of strategic interference. Within a marriage, sexual infidelity represents another form of strategic interference because it violates the desires of the spouse. Coercive control, threats, violence, insults, and attempts to lower a partner's self-esteem constitute other forms of strategic interference. The key point is that strategic interference, that is to say blocking the strategies and violating the desires of someone else, is predicted to pervade interactions between the sexes.

The second component of strategic interference theory postulates that the "negative" emotions such as anger, distress, and upset are psychological solutions that have evolved in part to solve the adaptive problems posed by strategic interference (Buss, 1989b). There are quotation marks around negative because although these emotions are generally painful to experience, they are hypothesised to be functional in solving the adaptive problems of strategic interference. First, they focus our attention on problematic events and momentarily screen out less relevant events. Attention is a scarce resource and must be allocated judiciously. When a person experiences anger or distress, these emotions guide his or her attention to the sources of the distress. Second, the emotions mark those events for storage in memory and easy retrieval from memory. Third, emotions lead to action, causing people to strive to eliminate the source of strategic interference or future interference.

In summary, the theory of strategic interference has two main postulates: (i) strategic interference is predicted to occur whenever members of one sex violate the desires of members of the opposite sex; historically, such interference would have prevented our forebears from successfully carrying out a preferred sexual strategy and hence would have reduced their reproductive success and

(ii) "negative" emotions such as anger, distress, jealousy and rage represent evolved solutions to the problems of strategic interference, alerting people to the sources of interference and prompting action designed to counteract it.

We must also note two important qualifiers: first, conflict per se serves no adaptive purpose. It is generally not adaptive for individuals to get into conflict with the opposite sex as an end in and of itself. Rather, conflict is typically an undesirable by-product of the fact that the sexual strategies of men and women differ in profound ways. Second, the metaphor of the "battle between the sexes" can be misleading: the phrase implies that men as a group are united in their interests and women are likewise united in their interests and that the two groups are somehow at war with each other. This is not the case nothing could be further from the truth. An evolutionary perspective helps us to understand why. Men cannot be united with all other men as a group for the fundamental reason that men compete primarily with other men. The same is true for women. Therefore, a unification or a "confluence of interests" cannot occur between all members of one sex. Of course, men and women can form specific alliances with particular members of their sex, but this in no way contradicts the fundamental principle that individuals are primarily in competition with members of their gender.

Violence

Mate retention has an extremely destructive side: the use of violence against partners.

Why would anyone ever commit violence against a partner? Wilson and Daly (1996) provide one hypothesis: men use violence and threats as a strategy to limit a partner's autonomy, decreasing the odds that the partner will commit infidelity or defect from the relationship. Indeed, women who leave their husbands are frequently assaulted, pursued, and threatened. Wives who have left their husbands are at greater risk of being killed than women who remain with their husbands. These spousal homicides often follow from threats to pursue and kill wives if they ever leave, and the murderers often explain their violent behaviour as a reaction to the unacceptable departure of their wives from the relationship (Wilson and Daly, 1996).

Intuitively, however, this homicidal behaviour seems bizarre and maladaptive. Killing a wife imposes a cost on the perpetrator as well as the victim, as the husband has essentially destroyed any access to a reproductively valuable asset. Killing a wife, therefore, seems genuinely puzzling from an evolutionary perspective. Wilson and Daly explain this puzzle by proposing that violence is a means of deterrence. Threats require credibility to be effective. Men, according to this logic, sometimes use violence to enhance the credibility of their threats. The violence, and even killing, seems quite counter to the man's self-interest. But, if the violence increases the credibility of the threats, then it can pay off, on average, when the man can subsequently use threats without resorting to actual violence. In short, the willingness to resort to extreme violence, according to this hypothesis, represents a risky strategy of deterring the wife from leaving and deterring sexual rivals: a strategy that sometimes has to be acted out to be effective.

Sexual jealousy in men predicts violence against their partners. One study of 116 couples assessed men's perceptions of their partners' interest in other men, as well as women's self-reported interest in other men (Cousins and Gangestad, 2007). Men's perceptions of their partner's interest in other men was a stronger predictor of male violence than women's actual interest in others. Another study found that men who accuse their partners of sexual infidelity are more prone to be physically violent toward them (Kaighobadi and Shackelford, 2009). Pregnant women seem especially vulnerable to abuse, especially if the man suspects that his partner might have become pregnant by another man (Buss and Duntley, 2011). A trio of studies found that men who devote a lot of effort to mate retention, particularly those who use the tactics of emotional manipulation and monopolization of the partner's time, are more likely to use physical violence to control their partner (Shackelford, Goetz, Buss, Euler, and Hoier, 2005). The presence of stepchildren in the home further increases the woman's risk of physical violence at his hands.

Another context that may provoke violence occurs when a man lacks the resources to provide positive incentives for a mate to remain in the relationship (Wilson and Daly, 1993). One study examined 1,156 women aged 16 or older who were killed in New York City over the 5 years 1990 through 1994 (Belluck, 1997). Nearly half were killed by husbands or boyfriends, either current or former. Approximately 67%, however, were killed in the poorest boroughs of New York: the Bronx and Brooklyn. The findings show higher rates of spousal homicide among men who are poor and unemployed: circumstances that prevent men from using positive incentives such as resource provisioning to keep a mate (Miner et al., 2009). Other factors that put women more at risk of violence from their partners include a proclivity toward short-term mating, psychopathic tendencies, and poor impulse control.

Personality characteristics are also predictors of the use of the more negative cost-inflicting mate-retention tactics. Although all three Dark Triad traits are linked with some cost-inflicting mate-retention tactics, psychopathy seems to be the strongest predictor (Jones and De Roos, 2017). Those high on psychopathy engage in more frequent verbal derogations of their mates, as well as threats and violence, particularly toward their intrasexual rivals. Interestingly, women high on Dark Triad traits are more likely to commit sexual infidelity while in relationships; and are also more likely to seek revenge on a partner who is unfaithful using verbal aggression and spreading bad rumours about their partner (Brewer, Hunt, James, & Abell, 2015). In contrast, the personality characteristics of agreeableness and conscientiousness are linked with benefit bestowing mate-retention actions, including love, attention, resources, and pleasuring a partner through oral sex (Sela, Shackelford, Pham, and Zeigler-Hill, 2015).

In summary, male sexual jealousy appears to be one of the central causes of violence against women within relationships. Violence appears to be used as a coercive tactic designed to keep a mate faithful, prevent future infidelity, and prevent departure from the relationship. Not all men use violence for these goals, and not all women are equally vulnerable. Men lacking the economic resources that might otherwise keep a woman in a relationship voluntarily are more prone to using violence. Young women, and hence high in reproductive value and attractive to other men, appear to be especially vulnerable to violent victimization by their partners. Two factors appear to reduce a woman's risk of violence: selecting a mate who has a reliable source of economic resources and having kin living close to her.

Bibliography

Baker, R. R., & Bellis, M. A. (1995). *Human sperm competition*. London: Chapman & Hall.

Barclay, P. (2010). Altruism as a courtship display: Some effects of third-party generosity on audience perceptions. *British Journal of Psychology, 101*, 123–135.

Belluck, P. (1997, March 31). *A woman's killer is likely to be her partner, a study finds.* New York Times.

Bendixen, M. (2014). Evidence of systematic bias in sexual over-and underperception of naturally occurring events: A direct replication of in a more gender-equal culture. *Evolutionary Psychology, 12* (5), 1004–1021.

Bendixen, M., & Kennair, L. E. O. (2017). Advances in the understanding of same-sex and opposite-sex sexual harassment. *Evolution and Human Behavior, 38* (5), 583–591.

Bereczkei, T., Gyuris, P., & Weisfeld, G. E. (2004). Sexual imprinting in human mate choice. *Proceedings of the Royal Society of London, B, 271*, 1129–1134. Berlin, B. (1992). Ethnobiological classification. Princeton, NJ: Princeton University Press.

Betzig, L. L. (1986). *Despotism and differential reproduction: A Darwinian view of history. Hawthorne*, NY: Aldine.

Betzig, L. L. (1989). Causes of conjugal dissolution. Current Anthropology, 30, 654–676. Betzig, L. L. (1992). Roman polygyny. *Ethology and Sociobiology, 13*, 309–349.

Bressler, E. R., Martin, R. A., & Balshine, S. (2006). Production and appreciation of humor as sexually selected traits. *Evolution and Human Behavior, 27,* 121–130.

Brewer, G., & Riley, C. (2009). Height, relationship satisfaction, jealousy, and mate retention. *Evolutionary Psychology, 7,* 477–489.

Brewer, G., Hunt, D., James, G., & Abell, L. (2015). Dark Triad traits, infidelity and romantic revenge. *Personality and Individual Differences, 83,* 122–127.

Bröder, A., & Hohmann, N. (2003). Variations in risk taking behavior over the menstrual cycle: An improved replication. *Evolution and Human Behavior, 24,* 391–398.

Brown, C. M., & Olkhov, Y. M. (2015). Functional flexibility in women's commitment-skepticism bias. *Evolutionary Psychology, 13* (2), 283–298.

Brown, D. E., & Chia-Yun, Y. (n.d.). *"Big man" as a statistical universal.* Santa Barbara, CA: Department of Anthropology, University of California.

Brown, M., & Sacco, D. F. (2018). Put a (limbal) ring on it: Women perceive men's limbal rings as a health cue in short-term mating domains. *Personality and Social Psychology Bulletin, 44* (1), 80–91.

Browne, K. R. (2002). *Biology at work: Rethinking sexual equality.* New Brunswick, NJ: Rutgers University Press.

Browne, K. R. (2006). Sex, power, and dominance: The evolutionary psychology of sexual harassment.

Managerial and Decision Economics, 27, 145–158.

Browne, K. R. (2010). The evolutionary psychology of sexual harassment. In J.D. Duntley & T. K. Shackelford (Eds.), *Evolutionary forensic psychology* (pp. 81–100). New York: Oxford University Press.

Burkett, B. N., & Cosmides, L. (2006, June). *What is intolerable in a mate?* Paper presented at the Annual Meeting of the Human Behavior and Evolution Society, Philadelphia, PA.

Burley, N., & Symanski, R. (1981). Women without: An evolutionary and cross-cultural perspective on prostitution. In R. Symanski (Ed.), *The immoral landscape: Female prostitution in Western societies* (pp. 239–274). Toronto: Butterworths.

Burnham, T. C., Chapman, J. F., Gray, P. B., McIntyre, M. H., Lipson, S. F., & Ellison, P. T. (2003). Men in committed, romantic relationships have lower testosterone. *Hormones and Behavior, 44*, 119–122.

Burriss, R. P., Welling, L. L., & Puts, D. A. (2011). Men's attractiveness predicts their preference for female facial femininity when judging for short-term, but not long-term, partners. *Personality and Individual Differences, 50* (5), 542–546.

Buss, D. M. (1989 b). Conflict between the sexes: Strategic interference and the evocation of anger and upset. *Journal of Personality and Social Psychology, 56*, 735–747.

Buss, D. M. (1991). Conflict in married couples: Personality predictors of anger and upset. *Journal of Personality, 59*, 663–688.

Buss, D. M. (1994b). *The evolution of desire: Strategies of human mating.* New York: Basic Books.

Buss, D. M. (1996a). Sexual conflict: Evolutionary insights into feminist and the "battle of the sexes." In D. M. Buss & N. M. Malamuth (Eds.), *Sex, power, conflict: Evolutionary and feminist perspectives* (pp. 296–318). New York: Oxford University Press.

Buss, D. M. (2003). *The evolution of desire: Strategies of human mating (Revised Edition).* New York: Free Press.

Buss, D. M. (2013, March). *Sexual double standards: The evolution of moral hypocrisy.* Talk presented at the Oakland Conference on the Evolution of Human Sexuality, Oaklan d, MI.

Buss, D. M. (2016b). *The evolution of desire: Strategies of human mating (revised and updated edition).* New York: Basic Books.

Buss, D. M., & Barnes, M. F. (1986). Preferences in human mate selection. *Journal of Personality and Social Psychology, 50*, 559–570.

Buss, D. M., & Duntley, J. D. (2011). The evolution of intimate partner violence. *Aggression and Violent Behavior, 16* (5), 411–419.

Buss, D. M., & Schmitt, D. P. (1993). Sexual strategies theory: An evolutionary perspective on human mating. *Psychological Review, 100*, 204–232.

Buss, D. M., & Shackelford, T. K. (1997c). From vigilance to violence: Mate retention tactics in married couples. *Journal of Personality and Social Psychology, 72*, 346–361.

Buss, D. M., & Shackelford, T. K. (2008). Attractive women want it all: Good genes, economic investment, parenting proclivities, and emotional commitment. *Evolutionary Psychology, 6*, 134–146.

Buss, D. M., Abbott, M., Angleitner, A., Asherian, A., Biaggio, A., & 45 other co-authors. (1990). International preferences in selecting mates: A study of 37 cultures. *Journal of Cross-Cultural Psychology, 21*, 5–47.

Buss, D. M., Goetz, C., Duntley, J. D., Asao, K., & Conroy-Beam, D. (2017). The mate switching hypothesis. *Personality and Individual Differences, 104*, 143–149.

Buss, D. M., Larsen, R., Westen, D., & Semmelroth, J. (1992). Sex differences in jealousy: Evolution, physiology, and psychology. *Psychological Science, 3*, 251–255.

Buss, D. M., Shackelford, T. K., Kirkpatrick, L. A., & Larsen, R. J. (2001). A half century of American mate preferences. *Journal of Marriage and the Family, 63*, 491–503.

Byers, E. S., & Lewis, K. (1988). Dating couples' disagreements over desired level of sexual intimacy. *Journal of Sex Research, 24*, 15–29.

Cameron, C., Oskamp, S., & Sparks, W. (1978). Courtship American style: Newspaper advertisements. *Family Coordinator, 26*, 27–30.

Camilleri, J. A., & Quinsey, V. L. (2009a). Testing the cuckoldry risk hypothesis of partner sexual coercion in community and forensic samples. *Evolutionary Psychology, 7*, 164–178.

Camilleri, J. A., & Quinsey, V. L. (2009b). Individual differences in the propensity for partner sexual coercion. *Sexual Abuse, 21*, 111–129.

Camilleri, J. A., Quinsey, V. L., & Tapscott, J. L. (2009). Assessing the propensity for sexual coaxing and coercion in relationships: Factor structure, reliability, and validity of the tactics to obtain sex scale. *Archives of Sexual Behavior, 38*, 959–973.

Campbell, L., Simpson, J. A., Stewart, M., & Manning, J. G. (2002). The formation of status hierarchies in leaderless groups: The role of male waist-to-hip ratio. *Human Nature, 13*, 345–362.

Castro, F. N., Hattori, W. T., & Lopes, F. (2012). Relationship maintenance or preference satisfaction? Male and female strategies in romantic partner choice. *Journal of Social, Evolutionary, and Cultural Psychology, 6*, 217–226.

Chavanne, T. J., & Gallup, G. G., Jr. (1998). Variation in risk taking behavior among female college students as a function of the menstrual cycle. *Evolution and Human Behavior, 19*, 27–32.

Colarelli, S. M., & Haaland, S. (2002). Perceptions of sexual harassment: An evolutionary perspective. Psychology, *Evolution, and Gender, 4*, 243–264.

Confer, J. C., Perilloux, C., & Buss, D. M. (2010). More than just a pretty face: Men's priority shifts toward bodily attractiveness in short-term mating contexts. *Evolution and Human Behavior, 31*, 349–353.

Cousins, A. J., & Gangestad, S. W. (2007). Perceived threats of female infidelity, male proprietariness, and violence in college dating couples. *Violence and Victims, 22*, 651–668.

Currie, T. E., & Little, A. C. (2009). The relative importance of the face and body in judgments of human attractiveness. *Evolution and Human Behavior, 30*, 409–416.

Cyrus, K., Schwarz, S., & Hassebrauck, M. (2011). Systematic cognitive biases in courtship context: Women's commitment—skepticism as a life-history strategy? *Evolution and Human Behavior, 32* (1), 13–20.

Daly, M., Wilson, M., & Weghorst, S. J. (1982). Male sexual jealousy. *Ethology and Sociobiology, 3*, 11–27.

DeSouza, E. R., Pierce, T., Zanelli, J. C., & Hutz, C. (1992). Perceived sexual intent in the U.S. and Brazil as a function of nature of encounter, subjects' nationality, and gender. *Journal of Sex Research, 29*, 251–260.

Dixon, A. F., Halliwell, G., East, R., Wignarajah, P., & Anderson, M. J. (2003). Masculine somatotype and hirsuteness as determinants of sexual attractiveness to women. *Archives of Sexual Behavior, 32*, 29–39.

Dunn, M. J., & Doria, M. V. (2010). Stimulated attraction increases sex attractiveness ratings in females but not males. *Journal of Social, Evolutionary, and Cultural Psychology, 4*, 1–17.

Dunn, M. J., & Hill, A. (2014). Manipulated luxury-apartment ownership enhances opposite-sex attraction in females but not males. *Journal of Evolutionary Psychology, 12*, 1–17.

Dunn, M. J., & Searle, R. (2010). Effect of manipulated prestige-car ownership on both sex attractiveness ratings. *British Journal of Psychology, 101*, 69– 80.

Ellis, B. J., & Symons, D. (1990). Sex differences in fantasy: An evolutionary psychological approach. *Journal of Sex Research, 27*, 527–556.

Ellis, L., Widmayer, A., & Palmer, C. T. (2009). Perpetrators of sexual assault continuing to have sex with their victims following the initial assault: Evidence for evolved reproductive strategies. *International Journal of Offender Therapy and Comparative Criminology, 53*, 454–463.

Faludi, S. (1991). Backlash: The undeclared war against American women. New York: Crown. Farrelly, D., Owens, R., Elliott, H. R., Walden, H. R., & Wetherell, M. A. (2015). The effects of being in a "new relationship" on levels of testosterone in men. *Evolutionary Psychology, 13* (1), 250–261.

Feinberg, D. R., Jones, B. C., Smith, M. J. L., Moore, F. R., DeBruine, L. M., Cronwell, R. E.,... & Perrett, D. I. (2006). Menstrual cycle, trait estrogen level, and masculinity preferences in the human voice. *Hormones and Behavior, 49*, 215–222.

Felson, R. B., & Cundiff, P. R. (2012). Age and sexual assault during robberies. *Evolution and Human Behavior, 33* (1), 10–16.

Fessler, D. M. T., & Navarrete, C. D. (2004). Third-party attitudes toward sibling incest: Evidence for

Westermarck's hypothesis. *Evolution and Human Behavior, 25,* 277–294.

Figueredo, A. J., Gladden, P. R., & Beck, C. J. A. (2010). Intimate partner violence and life history strategy. In A. Goetz & T. Shackelford (Eds.), *The Oxford handbook of sexual conflict in humans.* New York: Oxford University Press, 72–99.

Figueredo, A. J., Wolf, P. S. A., Olderbak, S. G., Sefcek, J. A., Frías-Armenta, M., Vargas-Porras, C., & Egan, V. (2015). Positive assortative pairing in social and romantic partners: A cross-cultural observational field study of naturally occurring pairs. *Personality and Individual Differences, 84,* 30–35.

Fisek, M. H., & Ofshe, R. (1970). The process of status evolution. *Sociometry, 33,* 327–346. Fisher, H. E. (1992). Anatomy of Love. New York: Norton.

Galperin, A., Haselton, M. G., Frederick, D. A., Poore, J., von Hippel, W., Buss, D. M., & Gonzaga, G. C. (2013). Sexual regret: Evidence for evolved sex differences. *Archives of Sexual Behavior, 42* (7), 1145–1161.

Gangestad, S. W., & Thornhill, R. (1997). Human sexual selection and developmental stability. In J. A. Simpson & D. T. Kenrick (Eds.), *Evolutionary social psychology* (pp. 169–195). Mahwah, NJ: Erlbaum.

Gangestad, S. W., Thornhill, R., & Garver-Apgar, C. E. (2005). Adaptations to ovulation. In D. M. Buss (Ed.), *The handbook of evolutionary psychology* (pp. 344–371). New York: Wiley.

Garcia, J. R., & Reiber, C. (2008). Hook-up behavior: A bio-psychosocial perspective. *Journal of Social, Evolutionary, and Cultural Psychology, 2*, 192–208.

Gladue, B. A., & Delaney, J. J. (1990). Gender differences in perception of attractiveness of men and women in bars. *Personality and Social Psychology Bulletin, 16*, 378–391.

Goetz, A. T., & Shackelford, T. K. (2009). Sexual coercion in intimate relationships: A comparative analysis of the effects of women's infidelity and men's dominance and control. *Archives of Sexual Behavior, 38*, 226– 234.

Goetz, C. D., Easton, J. A., Lewis, D. M. G., & Buss, D. M. (2012). Sexual exploitability: Observable cues and their link to sexual attraction. *Evolution and Human Behavior, 33*, 417–426.

Grammer, K. (1992). Variations on a theme: Age dependent mate selection in humans. *Behavioral and Brain Sciences, 15*, 100–102.

Gregor, T. (1985). *Anxious pleasures: The sexual lives of an Amazonian people*. Chicago, IL: University of Chicago Press.

Gutek, B. A. (1985). *Sex and the workplace: The impact of sexual behavior and harassment on women, men, and the organization*. San Francisco, CA: Jossey-Bass.

Hart, C. W., & Pilling, A. R. (1960). *The Tiwi of North Australia*. New York: Hart, Rinehart, & Winston.

Haselton, M. G. (2003). The sexual overperception bias: Evidence of a systematic bias in men from a survey of naturally occurring events. *Journal of Research in Personality, 37*, 34–47.

Haselton, M. G., & Buss, D. M. (2000). Error Management Theory: A new perspective on biases in cross-sex mind reading. *Journal of Personality and Social Psychology, 78*, 81–91.

Haselton, M. G., & Buss, D. M. (2001). The affective shift hypothesis: The functions of emotional changes following sexual intercourse. *Personal Relationships, 8*, 357–369.

Haselton, M. G., & Buss, D. M. (2003). Biases in social judgment: Design flaws or design features? In J. Forgas, W. von Hippel, & K. Williams (Eds.), *Responding to the social world: Explicit and implicit processes in social judgments and decisions* (pp. 23–43). Cambridge: Cambridge University Press.

Haselton, M. G., & Gangestad, S. G. (2006). Conditional expression of women's desires and men's mate guarding across the ovulation cycle. *Hormones and Behavior, 49*, 509–518.

Haselton, M. G., & Nettle, D. (2006). The paranoid optimist: An integrative evolutionary model of cognitive biases. *Personality and Social Psychology Review, 10*, 47–66.

Haselton, M. G., Buss, D. M., Oubaid, V., & Angleitner, A. (2005). Sex, lies, and strategic interference: The psychology of deception between the sexes. *Personality and Social Psychology Bulletin, 31*, 3–23.

Hawkes, K. (1991). Showing off: Tests of another hypothesis about men's foraging goals. *Ethology and Sociobiology, 11*, 29–54.

Hawkes, K., O'Connell, J. F., & Blurton Jones, N. G. (2001 a). Hunting and nuclear families. *Current Anthropology, 42*, 681–709.

Hawkes, K., O'Connell, J. F., & Blurton Jones, N. G. (2001 b). Hadza meat sharing. *Evolution and Human Behavior, 22*, 113–142.

Hill, S. E., & Buss, D. M. (2008a). The mere presence of opposite-sex others on judgments of sexual and romantic desirability: Opposite effects for men and women. *Personality and Social Psychology Bulletin, 34*, 635–647.

Holden, C. J., Zeigler-Hill, V., Pham, M. N., & Shackelford, T. K. (2014). Personality features and mate retention strategies: Honesty—humility and the willingness to manipulate, deceive, and exploit romantic partners. *Personality and Individual Differences, 57*, 31–36.

Hrdy, S. B. (1981). *The woman that never evolved.* Cambridge, MA: Harvard University Press.

Hughes, S. M., Harrison, M. A., & Gallup, G. G. Jr. (2004). Sex differences in mating strategies: Mate guarding, infidelity and multiple concurrent sex partners. *Sexualities, Evolution, and Gender, 6*, 3–13.

Jasienska, G., Ziomkiewicz, A., Ellison, P. T., Lipson, S. F., & Thune, I. (2004). Large breasts and narrow waists indicate high reproductive potential in women. *Proceedings of the Royal Society of London, B, 271*, 1213–1217.

Jencks, C. (1979). *Who gets ahead? The determinants of economic success in America*. New York: Basic Books.

Jonason, P. K., Garcia, J. R., Webster, G. D., Li, N. P., & Fisher, H. E. (2015). Relationship dealbreakers: Traits people avoid in potential mates. *Personality and Social Psychology Bulletin, 41 (12)*, 1697–1711.

Jonason, P. K., Li, N. P., & Buss, D. M. (2010). The costs and benefits of the Dark Triad: Implications for mate poaching and mate retention tactics. *Personality and Individual Differences, 48*, 373–378.

Jonason, P. K., Lyons, M., Baughman, H. M., & Vernon, P. A. (2014). What a tangled web we weave: The Dark Triad traits and deception. *Personality and Individual Differences, 70*, 117–119.

Jones, D. N., & De Roos, M. S. (2017). Machiavellian flexibility in negative mate retention. *Personal Relationships, 24* (2), 265–279.

Kaighobadi, F., & Shackelford, T. K. (2009). Suspicions of female infidelity predict men's partner-directed violence. *Behavioral and Brain Sciences, 32*, 281–282.

Kardum, I., Hudek-Knezevic, J., Schmitt, D. P., & Covic, M. (2017). Assortative mating for Dark Triad: Evidence of positive, initial, and active assortment. *Personal Relationships, 24* (1), 75–83.

Keenan, J. P., Gallup, G. G., Jr., Goulet, N., & Kulkarni, M. (1997). Attributions of deception in human mating strategies. *Journal of Social Behavior and Personality, 12*, 45–52.

Kennair, L. E. O., & Bendixen, M. (2012). Sociosexuality as predictor of sexual harassment and coercion in female and male high school students. *Evolution and Human Behavior, 33* (5), 479–490.

Kennair, L. E. O., Schmitt, D. P., Fjeldavli, Y. L., & Harlem, S. K. (2009). *Sex differences in sexual desires and attitudes in Norwegian samples*. Interpersona, 3 (Supplement 1), 1–32.

Kenrick, D. T., Keefe, R. C., Gabrielidis, C., & Cornelius, J. S. (1996). Adolescents age preferences for dating partners: Support for an evolutionary model of life-history strategies. *Child Development, 67*, 1499– 1511.

Kenrick, D. T., Neuberg, S. L., Zierk, K. L., & Krones, J. M. (1994). Evolution and social cognition: Contrast effects as a function of sex, dominance, and physical attractiveness. *Personality and Social Psychology Bulletin, 20*, 210–217.

Kinsey, A. C., Pomeroy, W. B., & Martin, C. E. (1948). *Sexual behavior in the human male*. Philadelphia, PA: Saunders.

Kinsey, A. C., Pomeroy, W. B., & Martin, C. E. (1953). *Sexual behavior in the human female*. Philadelphia, PA: Saunders.

Kohl, C., & Robertson, J. (2014). The sexual overperception bias: An exploration of the relationship between mate value and perception of sexual interest. *Evolutionary Behavioral Sciences, 8* (1), 31–43.

Kruger, D. J., Fisher, M., & Jobling, I. (2003). Proper and dark heroes as dads and cads: Alternative mating strategies in British romantic literature. *Human Nature, 14*, 305–317.

Kyl-Heku, L. M., & Buss, D. M. (1996). Tactics as units of analysis in personality psychology: An illustration using tactics of hierarchy negotiation. *Personality and Individual Differences, 21*, 497–517.

Lalumiere, M. L., Chalmers, L. J., Quinsey, V. L., & Seto, M. C. (1996). A test of the mate deprivation hypothesis of sexual coercion. *Ethology and Sociobiology, 17*, 299–318.

Lambert, T. A., Kahn, A. S., & Apple, K. J. (2003). Pluralistic ignorance and hooking up. *Journal of Sex Research, 40*, 129–133.

Langlois, J. H., & Roggman, L. A. (1990). Attractive faces are only average. *Psychological Science, 1*, 115–121.

Lenton, A. P., Bryan, A., Hastie, R., & Fischer, O. (2007). We want the same thing: Projection in judgments of sexual intent. *Personality and Social Psychology Bulletin, 33*, 975–988.

Li, N. P. (2007). Mate preference necessities in long- and short-term mating: People prioritize in themselves what their mates prioritize in them. *Acta Psychologica Sinica, 39*, 528–535.

Li, N. P., Griskevicius, V., Durante, K. M., Jonason, P. K., Pasisz, D. J., & Aumer, K. (2009). An evolutionary perspective on humor: Sexual selection or interest indication? *Personality and Social Psychology Bulletin, 35*, 923– 936.

Lieberman, D. (2009). Rethinking the Taiwanese minor marriage data: Evidence the mind uses multiple kinship cues to regulate inbreeding avoidance. *Evolution and Human Behavior, 30*, 153–160.

Lieberman, D., & Lobel, T. (2012). Kinship on the Kibbutz: Coresidence duration predicts altruism, personal sexual aversions and moral attitudes among communally reared peers. *Evolution and Human Behavior, 33*, 26– 34.

Lieberman, D., Tooby, J., & Cosmides, L. (2003). Does morality have a biological basis? An empirical test of the factors governing moral sentiments relating to incest. *Proceedings of the Royal Society of London, B, 270*, 819–826.

Lieberman, D., Tooby, J., & Cosmides, L. (2007). The architecture of human kin detection. *Nature, 445*, 727–731.

Lippa, R. A. (2009). Sex differences in sex drive, sociosexuality, and height across 53 nations: Testing evolutionary and social structural theories. *Archives of Sexual Behavior, 38*, 631– 651.

Little, A. C., Burriss, R. P., Jones, C., DeBruine, L. M., & Caldwell, C. A. (2008). Social influence in human face preference: Men and women are influenced more for long-term than short-term attractiveness decisions. *Evolution and Human Behavior, 29*, 140–146.

Little, A. C., Penton-Voak, I. S., Burt, D. M., & Perrett, D. I. (2002). Evolution and individual differences in the perception of attractiveness: How cyclic hormonal changes and self-perceived attractiveness influence female preferences for male faces. In G. Rhodes & L. A. Zebrowitz (Eds.), Facial attractiveness: *Evolutionary, cognitive, and social perspectives* (pp. 59–90). Westport, CT: Ablex.

Lukaszewski, A. W., & Roney, J. R. (2010). Kind toward whom? Mate preferences for personality traits are target specific. *Evolution and Human Behavior, 31*, 29–38.

Lund, O. C. H., Tamnes, C. K., Moestue, C., Buss, D. M., & Vollrath, M. (2007). Tactics of hierarchy negotiation. *Journal of Research in Personality, 41*, 25–44.

Maggioncalda, A. N., & Sapolsky, R. M. (2002). Disturbing behaviors of the orangutan. *Scientific American, 286*, 60–65.

Marlowe, F. W. (2005). Hunter-gatherers and human evolution. *Evolutionary Anthropology, 14*, 54–67.

Maynard Smith, J. (1982). *Evolution and the theory of games*. Cambridge: Cambridge University Press.

McDonald, M. M., Donnellan, M. B., Cesario, J., & Navarrete, C. D. (2015). Mate choice preferences in an intergroup context: Evidence for a sexual coercion threat-management system among women. *Evolution and Human Behavior, 36* (6), 438–445.

McKibbin, W. F., Shackelford, T. K., Goetz, A. T., & Starratt, V. G. (2008). Why do men rape? An evolutionary psychological perspective. *Review of General Psychology, 12*, 86–97.

McKibbin, W. F., Shackelford, T. K., Goetz, A. T., Bates, V. M., & Starrett, V.G. (2009). Developmental and initial psychometric assessment of the rape avoidance inventory. *Personality and Individual Differences, 46*, 336–340.

Miller, G. F. (2000). *The mating mind*. New York: Doubleday.

Miller, G. F. (2007). Sexual selection for moral virtues. *Quarterly Review of Biology, 82*, 97–125. Miller, G. F. (2009). Spent: Sex, evolution, and consumer behavior. New York: Viking.

Miner, E. J., Shackelford, T. K., & Starratt, V. G. (2009). Mate value of romantic partners predicts men's partner-directed verbal insults. *Personality and Individual Differences, 46*, 135–139.

Miner, E. J., Starratt, V. G., & Shackelford, T. K. (2009). It's not all about her: Men's mate value and mate retention. *Personality and Individual Differences, 47*, 214–218.

Nojo, S., Tamura, S., & Ihara, Y. (2012). Human homogamy in facial characteristics. *Human Nature, 23*, 323–340.

Owen, J., & Fincham, F. D. (2010). Effects of gender and psychosocial factors on "friends with benefits" relationship among young adults. *Archives of Sexual Behavior, 40* (2), 311–320. https://doi.org/10.1007/s10508-010-9611-6.

Paton, W., & Mannison, M. (1995). Sexual coercion in high school dating. *Sex Roles, 33*, 447–457.

Pawson, E., & Banks, G. (1993). Rape and fear in a New Zealand city. *Area, 25*, 55–63.

Perilloux, C., Easton, J. A., & Buss, D. M. (2012). The misperception of sexual interest. *Psychological Science, 23* (2), 146–151.

Petersen, J. L., & Hyde, J. S. (2010). A meta-analytic review of research on gender differences in sexuality, 1993–2007. *Psychological Bulletin, 136*, 21–38.

Phillips, T., Barnard, C., Ferguson, E., & Reader, T. (2008). Do humans prefer altruistic mates? Testing a link between sexual selection and altruism toward nonrelatives. *British Journal of Psychology, 99*, 555–572.

Pillsworth, E. G., Haselton, M. G., & Buss, D. M. (2004). Ovulatory shifts in female sexual desire. *Journal of Sex Research, 41*, 55–65.

Pisanski, K., & Feinberg, D. R. (2013). Cross-cultural variation in mate preferences for averageness, symmetry, body size, and masculinity. *Cross-Cultural Research, 47*, 162–197.

Poore, J. C., Haselton, M. G., von Hippel, W., & Buss, D. M. (2005, January). *Sexual regret*. Paper presented to the Annual Meeting of the Society of Personality and Social Psychologists, New Orleans.

Prokop, P. (2013). Rape avoidance behavior among Slovak women. *Evolutionary Psychology, 11* (2), 365–382.

Puts, D. A. (2005). Mating context and menstrual phase affect women's preferences for male voice pitch. *Evolution and Human Behavior, 26*, 388–397.

Puts, D. A., Dawood, K., & Welling, L. L. (2012). Why women have orgasms: An evolutionary analysis. *Archives of Sexual Behavior, 41* (5), 1127–1143.

Quinsey, V. L., & Lalumiere, M. L. (1995). Evolutionary perspectives on sexual offending. Sexual Abuse: A Journal of Research and Treatment, 7, 301–315. Raffield, B., Price, N., & Collard, M. (2017). Male-biased operational sex ratios and the Viking phenomenon: An evolutionary anthropological perspective on Late Iron Age Scandinavian raiding. *Evolution and Human Behavior, 38* (3), 315–324.

Rodeheffer, C. D., Proffitt Leyva, R. P., & Hill, S. E. (2016). Attractive female romantic partners provide a proxy for unobservable male qualities: The when and why behind human female mate choice copying. *Evolutionary Psychology, 14* (2), 1–8.

Roese, N. J., Pennington, G. L., Coleman, J., Janicki, M., Li, N. P., & Kenrick, D.T. (2006). Sex differences in regret: All for love or some for lust? *Personality and Social Psychology Bulletin, 32*, 770–780.

Roney, J. R. (2003). Effects of visual exposure to the opposite sex: Cognitive aspects of mate attraction in human males. *Personality and Social Psychology Bulletin, 29*, 393–404.

Sacco, D. F., Young, S. G., Brown, C. M., Bernstein, M. J., & Hugenberg, K. (2012). Social exclusion and female mating behavior: Rejected women show strategic enhancement of short-term mating interest. *Evolutionary Psychology, 10*, 573–587.

Schmitt, D. P. and 121 members of the International Sexuality Description Project. (2004). Patterns and universals of mate poaching across 53 nations: The effects of sex, culture, and personality on romantically attracting another person's partner. *Journal of Personality and Social Psychology, 86*, 560–584.

Schmitt, D. P., & Buss, D. M. (1996). Strategic self-promotion and competitor derogation: Sex and context effects on perceived effectiveness of mate attraction tactics. *Journal of Personality and Social Psychology, 70,* 1185– 1204.

Schmitt, D. P., & Buss, D. M. (2001). Human mate poaching: Tactics and temptations for infiltrating existing relationships. *Journal of Personality and Social Psychology, 80,* 894–917.

Schmitt, D. P., Shackelford, T. K., & Buss, D. M. (2001). Are men really more "oriented" toward short-term mating than women? *Psychology, Evolution, & Gender, 3,* 211–239.

Sela, Y., Shackelford, T. K., Pham, M. N., and Zeigler-Hill, V. (2015). Women's mate retention behaviors, personality traits, and fellatio. *Personality and Individual Differences, 85,* 187–191.

Shackelford, T. K., Goetz, A. T., Buss, D. M., Euler, H. A., & Hoier, S. (2005). When we hurt the ones we love: Predicting violence against women from men's mate retention. *Personal Relationships, 12,* 447–463.

Smith, E. A. (2004). Why do good hunters have higher reproductive success? *Human Nature, 15,* 343–364.

Smith, R. L. (1984). Human sperm competition. In R. L. Smith (Ed.), *Sperm competition and the evolution of mating systems* (pp. 601–659). New York: Academic Press.

Smuts, B. B. (1985). *Sex and friendship in baboons.* New York: Aldine de Gruyter.

Smuts, B. B. (1992). Men's aggression against women. *Human Nature, 6,* 1–32.

Smuts, B. B. (1995). The evolutionary origins of patriarchy. *Human Nature, 6,* 1–32.

Starratt, V. G., Popp, D., & Shackelford, T. K. (2008). Not all men are sexually coercive: A preliminary investigation of the moderating effect of mate desirability on the relationship between female infidelity and male sexual coercion. *Personality and Individual Differences, 45*, 10–14.

Studd, M. V., & Gattiker, U. E. (1991). The evolutionary psychology of sexual harassment in organizations. *Ethology and Sociobiology, 12*, 249–290.

Symons, D. (1979). *The evolution of human sexuality*. New York: Oxford.

Tanner, N. M. (1983). Hunters, gatherers, and sex roles in space and time. *American Anthropologist, 85*, 335–341.

Tanner, N. M., & Zihlman, A. (1976). Women in evolution part 1: Innovation and selection in human origins. Signs: *Women, Culture, and Society, 1*, 585–608.

ter Laak, J. J. F., Olthof, T., & Aleva, E. (2003). Sources of annoyance in close relationships: Sex-related differences in annoyance with partner behaviors. *The Journal of Psychology, 137*, 545–559.

Terpstra, D. E., & Cook, S. E. (1985). Complainant characteristics and reported behaviors and consequences associated with formal sexual harassment charges. *Personnel Psychology, 38*, 559–574.

Tessman, I. (1995). Human altruism as a courtship display. *Oikos, 74*, 157–158.

Thornhill, R. (1980). Rape in Panorpa scorpionflies and a general rape hypothesis. *Animal Behavior, 28*, 52–59.

Thornhill, R., & Palmer, C. (2000). *A natural history of rape: Biological bases of sexual coercion*. Cambridge, MA: MIT Press.

Thornhill, R., & Thornhill, N. (1983). Human rape: An evolutionary perspective. *Ethology and Sociobiology, 4*, 137–173.

Thornhill, R., & Thornhill, N. (1992). The evolutionary psychology of men's coercive sexuality. *Behavioral and Brain Sciences, 15*, 363–421.

Tooby, J., & DeVore, I. (1987). The reconstruction of hominid behavioral evolution through strategic modeling. In W. G. Kinzey (Ed.), *The evolution of human behavior* (pp. 183–237). New York: State University of New York Press.

Watkins, C. D., DeBruine, L. M., Smith, F. G., Jones, B. C., Vukovic, J., & Fraccaro, P. (2011). Like father, like self: Emotional closeness to father predicts women's preferences for self-resemblance in opposite-sex faces. *Evolution and Human Behavior, 32*, 70–75.

Waynforth, D. (2007). Mate choice copying in humans. *Human Nature, 18*, 264–271.

Waynforth, D., Delwadia, S., & Camm, M. (2005). The influence of women's mating strategies on preference for masculine facial architecture. *Evolution and Human Behavior, 26*, 409–416.

Willerman, L. (1979). *The psychology of individual and group differences*. San Francisco, CA: Freeman.

Wilson, G. D. (1987). Male–female differences in sexual activity, enjoyment, and fantasies. *Personality and Individual Differences, 8*, 125–126.

Wilson, G. D. (1997). Gender differences in sexual fantasy: An evolutionary analysis. *Personality and Individual Differences, 22*, 27–31.

Wilson, G. D., Cousins, J. M., & Fink, B. (2006). The CQ as a predictor of speed-date outcomes. *Sexual and Relationship Therapy, 21*, 163–169.

Wilson, M., & Daly, M. (1992). The man who mistook his wife for a chattel. In J. Barkow, L. Cosmides, & J. Tooby (Eds.), *The adapted mind: Evolutionary psychology and the generation of culture* (pp. 289–322). New York: Oxford University Press.

Wilson, M., & Daly, M. (1993). An evolutionary psychological perspective on male sexual proprietariness and violence against wives. *Violence and Victims, 8*, 271–294.

Wilson, M., & Daly, M. (1996). Male sexual proprietariness and violence against wives. *Current Directions in Psychological Science, 5*, 2–7.

Wilson, M., & Mesnick, S. L. (1997). An empirical test of the bodyguard hypothesis. In P. A. Gowaty (Ed.), *Feminism and evolutionary biology: Boundaries, intersections, and frontiers*. New York: Chapman & Hall, 505– 511.

Zeigler-Hill, V., Besser, A., Morag, J., & Campbell, W. K. (2016). The Dark Triad and sexual harassment proclivity. *Personality and Individual Differences, 89*, 47–54.

Zihlman, A. L. (1981). Women as shapers of the human adaptation. In F. Dahlberg (Ed.), *Woman the gatherer* (pp. 77–120). New Haven, CT: Yale University Press.

Credits

First Principles of Evolutionary Psychology

Maynard Smith, J. (1982). *Evolution and the theory of games*. Cambridge: Cambridge University Press.
Jasienska, G., Ziomkiewicz, A., Ellison, P. T., Lipson, S. F., & Thune, I. (2004). Large breasts and narrow waists indicate high reproductive potential in women. *Proceedings of the Royal Society of London, B, 271*, 1213–1217.

The Long-Term Mating Strategies of Men

Kenrick, D. T., Neuberg, S. L., Zierk, K. L., & Krones, J. M. (1994). Evolution and social cognition: Contrast effects as a function of sex, dominance, and physical attractiveness. *Personality and Social Psychology Bulletin, 20*, 210–217.
Buss, D. M., Shackelford, T. K., Kirkpatrick, L. A., & Larsen, R. J. (2001). A half century of American mate preferences. *Journal of Marriage and the Family, 63*, 491–503.
Grammer, K. (1992). Variations on a theme: Age dependent mate selection in humans. *Behavioral and Brain Sciences, 15*, 100–102.
Burriss, R. P., Welling, L. L., & Puts, D. A. (2011). Men's attractiveness predicts their preference for female facial femininity when judging for short-term, but not long-term, partners. *Personality and Individual Differences, 50* (5), 542–546.

Buss, D. M., & Schmitt, D. P. (1993). Sexual strategies theory: An evolutionary perspective on human mating. *Psychological Review, 100*, 204–232.

Langlois, J. H., & Roggman, L. A. (1990). Attractive faces are only average. *Psychological Science, 1*, 115–121.

Roney, J. R. (2003). Effects of visual exposure to the opposite sex: Cognitive aspects of mate attraction in human males. *Personality and Social Psychology Bulletin, 29*, 393–404.

Burnham, T. C., Chapman, J. F., Gray, P. B., McIntyre, M. H., Lipson, S. F., & Ellison, P. T. (2003). Men in committed, romantic relationships have lower testosterone. *Hormones and Behavior, 44*, 119–122.

Faludi, S. (1991). Backlash: The undeclared war against American women. New York: Crown. Farrelly, D., Owens, R., Elliott, H. R., Walden, H. R., & Wetherell, M. A. (2015). The effects of being in a "new relationship" on levels of testosterone in men. *Evolutionary Psychology, 13* (1), 250–261.

Tooby, J., & DeVore, I. (1987). The reconstruction of hominid behavioral evolution through strategic modeling. In W. G. Kinzey (Ed.), *The evolution of human behavior* (pp. 183–237). New York: State University of New York Press.

Hawkes, K., O'Connell, J. F., & Blurton Jones, N. G. (2001 a). Hunting and nuclear families. *Current Anthropology, 42*, 681–709.

Hawkes, K., O'Connell, J. F., & Blurton Jones, N. G. (2001 b). Hadza meat sharing. *Evolution and Human Behavior, 22*, 113–142.

Hawkes, K. (1991). Showing off: Tests of another hypothesis about men's foraging goals. *Ethology and Sociobiology, 11*, 29–54.

Smith, E. A. (2004). Why do good hunters have higher reproductive success? *Human Nature, 15*, 343–364.

Kenrick, D. T., Keefe, R. C., Gabrielidis, C., & Cornelius, J. S. (1996). Adolescents age preferences for dating partners: Support for an evolutionary model of life-history strategies. *Child Development, 67*, 1499– 1511.

The Long-Term Mating Strategies of Women

Jencks, C. (1979). *Who gets ahead? The determinants of economic success in America*. New York: Basic Books.

Willerman, L. (1979). *The psychology of individual and group differences*. San Francisco, CA: Freeman.

Kyl-Heku, L. M., & Buss, D. M. (1996). Tactics as units of analysis in personality psychology: An illustration using tactics of hierarchy negotiation. *Personality and Individual Differences, 21*, 497–517.

Lund, O. C. H., Tamnes, C. K., Moestue, C., Buss, D. M., & Vollrath, M. (2007). Tactics of hierarchy negotiation. *Journal of Research in Personality, 41*, 25–44.

Smuts, B. B. (1985). *Sex and friendship in baboons*. New York: Aldine de Gruyter.

Dixon, A. F., Halliwell, G., East, R., Wignarajah, P., & Anderson, M. J. (2003). Masculine somatotype and hirsuteness as determinants of sexual attractiveness to women. *Archives of Sexual Behavior, 32*, 29–39.

Buss, D. M., & Schmitt, D. P. (1993). Sexual strategies theory: An evolutionary perspective on human mating. *Psychological Review, 100*, 204–232.

Cameron, C., Oskamp, S., & Sparks, W. (1978). Courtship American style: Newspaper advertisements. *Family Coordinator, 26*, 27–30.

Hill, S. E., & Buss, D. M. (2008a). The mere presence of opposite-sex others on judgments of sexual and romantic desirability: Opposite effects for men and women. *Personality and Social Psychology Bulletin, 34*, 635–647.

Dunn, M. J., & Doria, M. V. (2010). Stimulated attraction increases sex attractiveness ratings in females but not males. *Journal of Social, Evolutionary, and Cultural Psychology, 4*, 1–17.

Waynforth, D. (2007). Mate choice copying in humans. *Human Nature, 18*, 264–271.

Little, A. C., Burriss, R. P., Jones, C., DeBruine, L. M., & Caldwell, C. A. (2008). Social influence in human face preference: Men and women are influenced more for long-term than short-term attractiveness decisions. *Evolution and Human Behavior, 29*, 140–146.

Rodeheffer, C. D., Proffitt Leyva, R. P., & Hill, S. E. (2016). Attractive female romantic partners provide a proxy for unobservable male qualities: The when and why behind human female mate choice copying. *Evolutionary Psychology, 14* (2), 1–8.

Buss, D. M., Abbott, M., Angleitner, A., Asherian, A., Biaggio, A., & 45 other co-authors. (1990).

International preferences in selecting mates: A study of 37 cultures. *Journal of Cross-Cultural Psychology, 21*, 5–47.

Buss, D. M. (1991). Conflict in married couples: Personality predictors of anger and upset. *Journal of Personality, 59*, 663–688.

Buss, D. M., Shackelford, T. K., Kirkpatrick, L. A., & Larsen, R. J. (2001). A half century of American mate preferences. *Journal of Marriage and the Family, 63*, 491–503.

Betzig, L. L. (1986). *Despotism and differential reproduction: A Darwinian view of history. Hawthorne*, NY: Aldine.

Brown, D. E., & Chia-Yun, Y. (n.d.). *"Big man" as a statistical universal.* Santa Barbara, CA: Department of Anthropology, University of California.

Li, N. P. (2007). Mate preference necessities in long- and short-term mating: People prioritize in themselves what their mates prioritize in them. *Acta Psychologica Sinica, 39*, 528–535.

Dunn, M. J., & Searle, R. (2010). Effect of manipulated prestige-car ownership on both sex attractiveness ratings. *British Journal of Psychology, 101*, 69– 80.

Dunn, M. J., & Hill, A. (2014). Manipulated luxury-apartment ownership enhances opposite-sex attraction in females but not males. *Journal of Evolutionary Psychology, 12*, 1–17.

Lieberman, D., Tooby, J., & Cosmides, L. (2003). Does morality have a biological basis? An empirical test of the factors governing moral sentiments relating to incest. *Proceedings of the Royal Society of London, B, 270*, 819–826.

Fessler, D. M. T., & Navarrete, C. D. (2004). Third-party attitudes toward sibling incest: Evidence for Westermarck's hypothesis. *Evolution and Human Behavior, 25*, 277–294.

Lieberman, D., Tooby, J., & Cosmides, L. (2007). The architecture of human kin detection. *Nature, 445*, 727–731.

Lieberman, D. (2009). Rethinking the Taiwanese minor marriage data: Evidence the mind uses multiple kinship cues to regulate inbreeding avoidance. *Evolution and Human Behavior, 30*, 153–160.

Lieberman, D., & Lobel, T. (2012). Kinship on the Kibbutz: Coresidence duration predicts altruism, personal sexual aversions and moral attitudes among communally reared peers. *Evolution and Human Behavior, 33*, 26– 34.

Burkett, B. N., & Cosmides, L. (2006, June). *What is intolerable in a mate?* Paper presented at the Annual Meeting of the Human Behavior and Evolution Society, Philadelphia, PA.

Jonason, P. K., Garcia, J. R., Webster, G. D., Li, N. P., & Fisher, H. E. (2015). Relationship dealbreakers: Traits people avoid in potential mates. *Personality and Social Psychology Bulletin, 41 (12)*, 1697–1711.

Phillips, T., Barnard, C., Ferguson, E., & Reader, T. (2008). Do humans prefer altruistic mates? Testing a link between sexual selection and altruism toward nonrelatives. *British Journal of Psychology, 99*, 555–572.

Barclay, P. (2010). Altruism as a courtship display: Some effects of third-party generosity on audience perceptions. *British Journal of Psychology, 101,* 123–135.

Lukaszewski, A. W., & Roney, J. R. (2010). Kind toward whom? Mate preferences for personality traits are target specific. *Evolution and Human Behavior, 31,* 29–38.

Miller, G. F. (2007). Sexual selection for moral virtues. *Quarterly Review of Biology, 82,* 97–125. Miller, G. F. (2009). Spent: Sex, evolution, and consumer behavior. New York: Viking.

Buss, D. M. (2016b). *The evolution of desire: Strategies of human mating (revised and updated edition).* New York: Basic Books.

Tessman, I. (1995). Human altruism as a courtship display. *Oikos, 74,* 157–158.

Buss, D. M., & Shackelford, T. K. (2008). Attractive women want it all: Good genes, economic investment, parenting proclivities, and emotional commitment. *Evolutionary Psychology, 6,* 134–146.

Buss, D. M., & Barnes, M. F. (1986). Preferences in human mate selection. *Journal of Personality and Social Psychology, 50,* 559–570.

Miller, G. F. (2000). *The mating mind.* New York: Doubleday.

Bressler, E. R., Martin, R. A., & Balshine, S. (2006). Production and appreciation of humor as sexually selected traits. *Evolution and Human Behavior, 27,* 121–130.

Li, N. P., Griskevicius, V., Durante, K. M., Jonason, P. K., Pasisz, D. J., & Aumer, K. (2009). An evolutionary perspective on humor: Sexual selection or interest indication? *Personality and Social Psychology Bulletin, 35*, 923– 936.

Puts, D. A. (2005). Mating context and menstrual phase affect women's preferences for male voice pitch. *Evolution and Human Behavior, 26*, 388–397.

Hart, C. W., & Pilling, A. R. (1960). *The Tiwi of North Australia*. New York: Hart, Rinehart, & Winston.

Buss, D. M. (2003). *The evolution of desire: Strategies of human mating (Revised Edition)*. New York: Free Press.

Castro, F. N., Hattori, W. T., & Lopes, F. (2012). Relationship maintenance or preference satisfaction? Male and female strategies in romantic partner choice. *Journal of Social, Evolutionary, and Cultural Psychology, 6*, 217–226.

Wilson, G. D., Cousins, J. M., & Fink, B. (2006). The CQ as a predictor of speed-date outcomes. *Sexual and Relationship Therapy, 21*, 163–169.

Kardum, I., Hudek-Knezevic, J., Schmitt, D. P., & Covic, M. (2017). Assortative mating for Dark Triad: Evidence of positive, initial, and active assortment. *Personal Relationships, 24* (1), 75–83.

Bereczkei, T., Gyuris, P., & Weisfeld, G. E. (2004). Sexual imprinting in human mate choice. *Proceedings of the Royal Society of London, B, 271*, 1129–1134. Berlin, B. (1992). Ethnobiological classification. Princeton, NJ: Princeton University Press.

Watkins, C. D., DeBruine, L. M., Smith, F. G., Jones, B. C., Vukovic, J., & Fraccaro, P. (2011). Like father, like self: Emotional closeness to father predicts women's preferences for self-resemblance in opposite-sex faces. *Evolution and Human Behavior, 32*, 70–75.

Nojo, S., Tamura, S., & Ihara, Y. (2012). Human homogamy in facial characteristics. *Human Nature, 23*, 323–340.

Figueredo, A. J., Wolf, P. S. A., Olderbak, S. G., Sefcek, J. A., Frías-Armenta, M., Vargas-Porras, C., & Egan, V. (2015). Positive assortative pairing in social and romantic partners: A cross-cultural observational field study of naturally occurring pairs. *Personality and Individual Differences, 84*, 30–35.

Schmitt, D. P., & Buss, D. M. (1996). Strategic self-promotion and competitor derogation: Sex and context effects on perceived effectiveness of mate attraction tactics. *Journal of Personality and Social Psychology, 70,* 1185– 1204.

Tanner, N. M., & Zihlman, A. (1976). Women in evolution part 1: Innovation and selection in human origins. Signs: *Women, Culture, and Society, 1*, 585–608.

Zihlman, A. L. (1981). Women as shapers of the human adaptation. In F. Dahlberg (Ed.), *Woman the gatherer* (pp. 77–120). New Haven, CT: Yale University Press.

Tanner, N. M. (1983). Hunters, gatherers, and sex roles in space and time. *American Anthropologist, 85*, 335–341.

Marlowe, F. W. (2005). Hunter-gatherers and human evolution. *Evolutionary Anthropology, 14,* 54–67.

Little, A. C., Penton-Voak, I. S., Burt, D. M., & Perrett, D. I. (2002). Evolution and individual differences in the perception of attractiveness: How cyclic hormonal changes and self-perceived attractiveness influence female preferences for male faces. In G. Rhodes & L. A. Zebrowitz (Eds.), Facial attractiveness: *Evolutionary, cognitive, and social perspectives* (pp. 59–90). Westport, CT: Ablex.

Feinberg, D. R., Jones, B. C., Smith, M. J. L., Moore, F. R., DeBruine, L. M., Cronwell, R. E.,... & Perrett, D. I. (2006). Menstrual cycle, trait estrogen level, and masculinity preferences in the human voice. *Hormones and Behavior, 49,* 215–222.

Pisanski, K., & Feinberg, D. R. (2013). Cross-cultural variation in mate preferences for averageness, symmetry, body size, and masculinity. *Cross-Cultural Research, 47,* 162–197.

The Short-Term Mating Strategies of the Sexes

Kinsey, A. C., Pomeroy, W. B., & Martin, C. E. (1948). *Sexual behavior in the human male*. Philadelphia, PA: Saunders.

Kinsey, A. C., Pomeroy, W. B., & Martin, C. E. (1953). *Sexual behavior in the human female*. Philadelphia, PA: Saunders.

Gregor, T. (1985). *Anxious pleasures: The sexual lives of an Amazonian people*.

Smith, R. L. (1984). Human sperm competition. In R. L. Smith (Ed.), *Sperm competition and the evolution of mating systems* (pp. 601–659). New York: Academic Press.

Gangestad, S. W., & Thornhill, R. (1997). Human sexual selection and developmental stability. In J. A. Simpson & D. T. Kenrick (Eds.), *Evolutionary social psychology* (pp. 169–195). Mahwah, NJ: Erlbaum.

Kruger, D. J., Fisher, M., & Jobling, I. (2003). Proper and dark heroes as dads and cads: Alternative mating strategies in British romantic literature. *Human Nature, 14*, 305–317.

Waynforth, D., Delwadia, S., & Camm, M. (2005). The influence of women's mating strategies on preference for masculine facial architecture. *Evolution and Human Behavior, 26*, 409–416.

Sacco, D. F., Young, S. G., Brown, C. M., Bernstein, M. J., & Hugenberg, K. (2012). Social exclusion and female mating behavior: Rejected women show strategic enhancement of short-term mating interest. *Evolutionary Psychology, 10*, 573–587.

Brown, M., & Sacco, D. F. (2018). Put a (limbal) ring on it: Women perceive men's limbal rings as a health cue in short-term mating domains. *Personality and Social Psychology Bulletin, 44* (1), 80–91.

Owen, J., & Fincham, F. D. (2010). Effects of gender and psychosocial factors on "friends with benefits" relationship among young adults. *Archives of Sexual Behavior, 40* (2), 311–320. https://doi.org/10.1007/s10508-010-9611-6.

Garcia, J. R., & Reiber, C. (2008). Hook-up behavior: A bio-psychosocial perspective. *Journal of Social, Evolutionary, and Cultural Psychology, 2*, 192–208.

Campbell, L., Simpson, J. A., Stewart, M., & Manning, J. G. (2002). The formation of status hierarchies in leaderless groups: The role of male waist-to-hip ratio. *Human Nature, 13*, 345–362.

Buss, D. M., & Schmitt, D. P. (1993). Sexual strategies theory: An evolutionary perspective on human mating. *Psychological Review, 100*, 204–232.

Currie, T. E., & Little, A. C. (2009). The relative importance of the face and body in judgments of human attractiveness. *Evolution and Human Behavior, 30*, 409–416.

Confer, J. C., Perilloux, C., & Buss, D. M. (2010). More than just a pretty face: Men's priority shifts toward bodily attractiveness in short-term mating contexts. *Evolution and Human Behavior, 31*, 349–353.

Betzig, L. L. (1989). Causes of conjugal dissolution. Current Anthropology, 30, 654–676. Betzig, L. L. (1992). Roman polygyny. *Ethology and Sociobiology, 13*, 309–349.

Fisek, M. H., & Ofshe, R. (1970). The process of status evolution. *Sociometry, 33*, 327–346. Fisher, H. E. (1992). Anatomy of Love. New York: Norton.

Buss, D. M., Goetz, C., Duntley, J. D., Asao, K., & Conroy-Beam, D. (2017). The mate switching hypothesis. *Personality and Individual Differences, 104*, 143–149.

Baker, R. R., & Bellis, M. A. (1995). *Human sperm competition*. London: Chapman & Hall.

Puts, D. A., Dawood, K., & Welling, L. L. (2012). Why women have orgasms: An evolutionary analysis. *Archives of Sexual Behavior, 41* (5), 1127–1143.

Symons, D. (1979). *The evolution of human sexuality*. New York: Oxford.

Burley, N., & Symanski, R. (1981). Women without: An evolutionary and cross-cultural perspective on prostitution. In R. Symanski (Ed.), *The immoral landscape: Female prostitution in Western societies* (pp. 239–274). Toronto: Butterworths.

Hrdy, S. B. (1981). *The woman that never evolved*. Cambridge, MA: Harvard University Press.

Smuts, B. B. (1985). *Sex and friendship in baboons*. New York: Aldine de Gruyter.

Wilson, G. D. (1987). Male–female differences in sexual activity, enjoyment, and fantasies. *Personality and Individual Differences, 8*, 125–126.

Ellis, B. J., & Symons, D. (1990). Sex differences in fantasy: An evolutionary psychological approach. *Journal of Sex Research, 27*, 527–556.

Wilson, G. D. (1997). Gender differences in sexual fantasy: An evolutionary analysis. *Personality and Individual Differences, 22*, 27–31.

Hughes, S. M., Harrison, M. A., & Gallup, G. G. Jr. (2004). Sex differences in mating strategies: Mate guarding, infidelity and multiple concurrent sex partners. *Sexualities, Evolution, and Gender, 6*, 3–13.

Lippa, R. A. (2009). Sex differences in sex drive, sociosexuality, and height across 53 nations:

Testing evolutionary and social structural theories. *Archives of Sexual Behavior, 38*, 631–651.

Petersen, J. L., & Hyde, J. S. (2010). A meta-analytic review of research on gender differences in sexuality, 1993–2007. *Psychological Bulletin, 136*, 21–38.

Goetz, C. D., Easton, J. A., Lewis, D. M. G., & Buss, D. M. (2012). Sexual exploitability: Observable cues and their link to sexual attraction. *Evolution and Human Behavior, 33*, 417–426.

Poore, J. C., Haselton, M. G., von Hippel, W., & Buss, D. M. (2005, January). *Sexual regret*. Paper presented to the Annual Meeting of the Society of Personality and Social Psychologists, New Orleans.

Roese, N. J., Pennington, G. L., Coleman, J., Janicki, M., Li, N. P., & Kenrick, D.T. (2006). Sex differences in regret: All for love or some for lust? *Personality and Social Psychology Bulletin, 32*, 770–780.

Galperin, A., Haselton, M. G., Frederick, D. A., Poore, J., von Hippel, W., Buss, D. M., & Gonzaga, G. C. (2013). Sexual regret: Evidence for evolved sex differences. *Archives of Sexual Behavior, 42* (7), 1145–1161.

Lambert, T. A., Kahn, A. S., & Apple, K. J. (2003). Pluralistic ignorance and hooking up. *Journal of Sex Research, 40*, 129–133.

Haselton, M. G., & Buss, D. M. (2001). The affective shift hypothesis: The functions of emotional changes following sexual intercourse. *Personal Relationships, 8*, 357–369.

Gladue, B. A., & Delaney, J. J. (1990). Gender differences in perception of attractiveness of men and women in bars. *Personality and Social Psychology Bulletin, 16*, 378–391.

Schmitt, D. P., Shackelford, T. K., & Buss, D. M. (2001). Are men really more "oriented" toward short-term mating than women? *Psychology, Evolution, & Gender, 3*, 211–239.

Kennair, L. E. O., Schmitt, D. P., Fjeldavli, Y. L., & Harlem, S. K. (2009). *Sex differences in sexual desires and attitudes in Norwegian samples*. Interpersona, 3 (Supplement 1), 1–32.

Conflicts Between the Sexes

Buss, D. M. (2003). *The evolution of desire: Strategies of human mating (Revised Edition)*. New York: Free Press.

Gregor, T. (1985). *Anxious pleasures: The sexual lives of an Amazonian people*. Chicago, IL: University of Chicago Press.

Smuts, B. B. (1992). Men's aggression against women. *Human Nature, 6*, 1–32.

Wilson, M., & Mesnick, S. L. (1997). An empirical test of the bodyguard hypothesis. In P. A. Gowaty (Ed.), *Feminism and evolutionary biology: Boundaries, intersections, and frontiers*. New York: Chapman & Hall, 505– 511.

Chavanne, T. J., & Gallup, G. G., Jr. (1998). Variation in risk taking behavior among female college students as a function of the menstrual cycle. *Evolution and Human Behavior, 19*, 27–32.

Thornhill, R., & Palmer, C. (2000). *A natural history of rape: Biological bases of sexual coercion*. Cambridge, MA: MIT Press.

Bröder, A., & Hohmann, N. (2003). Variations in risk taking behavior over the menstrual cycle: An improved replication. *Evolution and Human Behavior, 24*, 391–398.

McDonald, M. M., Donnellan, M. B., Cesario, J., & Navarrete, C. D. (2015). Mate choice preferences in an intergroup context: Evidence for a sexual coercion threat-management system among women. *Evolution and Human Behavior, 36* (6), 438–445.

Pawson, E., & Banks, G. (1993). Rape and fear in a New Zealand city. *Area, 25*, 55–63.

Prokop, P. (2013). Rape avoidance behavior among Slovak women. *Evolutionary Psychology, 11* (2), 365–382.

McKibbin, W. F., Shackelford, T. K., Goetz, A. T., Bates, V. M., & Starrett, V.G. (2009). Developmental and initial psychometric assessment of the rape avoidance inventory. *Personality and Individual Differences, 46*, 336–340.

Haselton, M. G. (2003). The sexual overperception bias: Evidence of a systematic bias in men from a survey of naturally occurring events. *Journal of Research in Personality, 37*, 34–47.

Haselton, M. G., & Buss, D. M. (2000). Error Management Theory: A new perspective on biases in cross-sex mind reading. *Journal of Personality and Social Psychology, 78*, 81–91.

Haselton, M. G., & Buss, D. M. (2003). Biases in social judgment: Design flaws or design features? In J. Forgas, W. von Hippel, & K. Williams (Eds.), *Responding to the social world: Explicit and implicit processes in social judgments and decisions* (pp. 23–43). Cambridge: Cambridge University Press.

Haselton, M. G., & Nettle, D. (2006). The paranoid optimist: An integrative evolutionary model of cognitive biases. *Personality and Social Psychology Review, 10*, 47–66.

Lenton, A. P., Bryan, A., Hastie, R., & Fischer, O. (2007). We want the same thing: Projection in judgments of sexual intent. *Personality and Social Psychology Bulletin, 33*, 975–988.

Perilloux, C., Easton, J. A., & Buss, D. M. (2012). The misperception of sexual interest. *Psychological Science, 23* (2), 146–151.

Kohl, C., & Robertson, J. (2014). The sexual overperception bias: An exploration of the relationship between mate value and perception of sexual interest. *Evolutionary Behavioral Sciences, 8* (1), 31–43.

Haselton, M. G., Buss, D. M., Oubaid, V., & Angleitner, A. (2005). Sex, lies, and strategic interference: The psychology of deception between the sexes. *Personality and Social Psychology Bulletin, 31*, 3–23.

Keenan, J. P., Gallup, G. G., Jr., Goulet, N., & Kulkarni, M. (1997). Attributions of deception in human mating strategies. *Journal of Social Behavior and Personality, 12*, 45–52.

Brown, C. M., & Olkhov, Y. M. (2015). Functional flexibility in women's commitment-skepticism bias. *Evolutionary Psychology, 13* (2), 283–298.

Cyrus, K., Schwarz, S., & Hassebrauck, M. (2011). Systematic cognitive biases in courtship context: Women's commitment—skepticism as a life-history strategy? *Evolution and Human Behavior, 32* (1), 13–20.

Buss, D. M. (1994b). *The evolution of desire: Strategies of human mating.* New York: Basic Books.

Jonason, P. K., Lyons, M., Baughman, H. M., & Vernon, P. A. (2014). What a tangled web we weave: The Dark Triad traits and deception. *Personality and Individual Differences, 70*, 117–119.

Thornhill, R. (1980). Rape in Panorpa scorpionflies and a general rape hypothesis. *Animal Behavior, 28*, 52–59.

Maggioncalda, A. N., & Sapolsky, R. M. (2002). Disturbing behaviors of the orangutan. *Scientific American, 286*, 60–65.

Symons, D. (1979). *The evolution of human sexuality.* New York: Oxford.

Thornhill, R., & Thornhill, N. (1983). Human rape: An evolutionary perspective. *Ethology and Sociobiology, 4*, 137–173.

Felson, R. B., & Cundiff, P. R. (2012). Age and sexual assault during robberies. *Evolution and Human Behavior, 33* (1), 10–16.

Buss, D. M., & Shackelford, T. K. (1997c). From vigilance to violence: Mate retention tactics in married couples. *Journal of Personality and Social Psychology, 72*, 346–361.

Brewer, G., & Riley, C. (2009). Height, relationship satisfaction, jealousy, and mate retention. *Evolutionary Psychology, 7*, 477–489.

Miner, E. J., Shackelford, T. K., & Starratt, V. G. (2009). Mate value of romantic partners predicts men's partner-directed verbal insults. *Personality and Individual Differences, 46*, 135–139.

Miner, E. J., Starratt, V. G., & Shackelford, T. K. (2009). It's not all about her: Men's mate value and mate retention. *Personality and Individual Differences, 47*, 214–218.

Jonason, P. K., Li, N. P., & Buss, D. M. (2010). The costs and benefits of the Dark Triad: Implications for mate poaching and mate retention tactics. *Personality and Individual Differences, 48*, 373–378.

Holden, C. J., Zeigler-Hill, V., Pham, M. N., & Shackelford, T. K. (2014). Personality features and mate retention strategies: Honesty—humility and the willingness to manipulate, deceive, and exploit romantic partners. *Personality and Individual Differences, 57*, 31–36.

Schmitt, D. P., & Buss, D. M. (2001). Human mate poaching: Tactics and temptations for infiltrating existing relationships. *Journal of Personality and Social Psychology, 80*, 894–917.

Schmitt, D. P. and 121 members of the International Sexuality Description Project. (2004). Patterns and universals of mate poaching across 53 nations: The effects of sex, culture, and personality on romantically attracting another person's partner. *Journal of Personality and Social Psychology, 86*, 560–584.

Daly, M., Wilson, M., & Weghorst, S. J. (1982). Male sexual jealousy. *Ethology and Sociobiology, 3*, 11–27.

Buss, D. M. (2013, March). *Sexual double standards: The evolution of moral hypocrisy*. Talk presented at the Oakland Conference on the Evolution of Human Sexuality, Oaklan d, MI.

Buss, D. M., Larsen, R., Westen, D., & Semmelroth, J. (1992). Sex differences in jealousy: Evolution, physiology, and psychology. *Psychological Science, 3*, 251–255.

Thornhill, R., & Thornhill, N. (1992). The evolutionary psychology of men's coercive sexuality. *Behavioral and Brain Sciences, 15*, 363–421.

Quinsey, V. L., & Lalumiere, M. L. (1995). Evolutionary perspectives on sexual offending. Sexual Abuse: A Journal of Research and Treatment, 7, 301–315. Raffield, B., Price, N., & Collard, M. (2017). Male-biased operational sex ratios and the Viking phenomenon: An evolutionary anthropological perspective on Late Iron Age Scandinavian raiding. *Evolution and Human Behavior, 38* (3), 315–324.

Lalumiere, M. L., Chalmers, L. J., Quinsey, V. L., & Seto, M. C. (1996). A test of the mate deprivation hypothesis of sexual coercion. *Ethology and Sociobiology, 17*, 299–318.

Camilleri, J. A., Quinsey, V. L., & Tapscott, J. L. (2009). Assessing the propensity for sexual coaxing and coercion in relationships: Factor structure, reliability, and validity of the tactics to obtain sex scale. *Archives of Sexual Behavior, 38*, 959–973.

Ellis, L., Widmayer, A., & Palmer, C. T. (2009). Perpetrators of sexual assault continuing to have sex with their victims following the initial assault: Evidence for evolved reproductive strategies. *International Journal of Offender Therapy and Comparative Criminology, 53*, 454–463.

Byers, E. S., & Lewis, K. (1988). Dating couples' disagreements over desired level of sexual intimacy. *Journal of Sex Research, 24*, 15–29.

Paton, W., & Mannison, M. (1995). Sexual coercion in high school dating. *Sex Roles, 33*, 447–457.

Gangestad, S. W., Thornhill, R., & Garver-Apgar, C. E. (2005). Adaptations to ovulation. In D. M. Buss (Ed.), *The handbook of evolutionary psychology* (pp. 344–371). New York: Wiley.

Haselton, M. G., & Gangestad, S. G. (2006). Conditional expression of women's desires and men's mate guarding across the ovulation cycle. *Hormones and Behavior, 49*, 509–518.

Pillsworth, E. G., Haselton, M. G., & Buss, D. M. (2004). Ovulatory shifts in female sexual desire. *Journal of Sex Research, 41*, 55–65.

McKibbin, W. F., Shackelford, T. K., Goetz, A. T., & Starratt, V. G. (2008). Why do men rape? An evolutionary psychological perspective. *Review of General Psychology, 12*, 86–97.

Goetz, A. T., & Shackelford, T. K. (2009). Sexual coercion in intimate relationships: A comparative analysis of the effects of women's infidelity and men's dominance and control. *Archives of Sexual Behavior, 38*, 226– 234.

Camilleri, J. A., & Quinsey, V. L. (2009a). Testing the cuckoldry risk hypothesis of partner sexual coercion in community and forensic samples. *Evolutionary Psychology, 7*, 164–178.

Camilleri, J. A., & Quinsey, V. L. (2009b). Individual differences in the propensity for partner sexual coercion. *Sexual Abuse, 21*, 111–129.

Figueredo, A. J., Gladden, P. R., & Beck, C. J. A. (2010). Intimate partner violence and life history strategy. In A. Goetz & T. Shackelford (Eds.), *The Oxford handbook of sexual conflict in humans.* New York: Oxford University Press, 72–99.

Starratt, V. G., Popp, D., & Shackelford, T. K. (2008). Not all men are sexually coercive: A preliminary investigation of the moderating effect of mate desirability on the relationship between female infidelity and male sexual coercion. *Personality and Individual Differences, 45*, 10–14.

Tooby, J., & DeVore, I. (1987). The reconstruction of hominid behavioral evolution through strategic modeling. In W. G. Kinzey (Ed.), *The evolution of human behavior* (pp. 183–237). New York: State University of New York Press.

Wilson, M., & Daly, M. (1992). The man who mistook his wife for a chattel. In J. Barkow, L. Cosmides, & J. Tooby (Eds.), *The adapted mind: Evolutionary psychology and the generation of culture* (pp. 289–322). New York: Oxford University Press.

Buss, D. M. (1996a). Sexual conflict: Evolutionary insights into feminist and the "battle of the sexes." In D. M. Buss & N. M. Malamuth (Eds.), *Sex, power, conflict: Evolutionary and feminist perspectives* (pp. 296–318). New York: Oxford University Press.

Smuts, B. B. (1995). The evolutionary origins of patriarchy. *Human Nature, 6*, 1–32.

Buss, D. M. (1989 b). Conflict between the sexes: Strategic interference and the evocation of anger and upset. *Journal of Personality and Social Psychology, 56*, 735–747.

ter Laak, J. J. F., Olthof, T., & Aleva, E. (2003). Sources of annoyance in close relationships: Sex-related differences in annoyance with partner behaviors. *The Journal of Psychology, 137*, 545–559.

Terpstra, D. E., & Cook, S. E. (1985). Complainant characteristics and reported behaviors and consequences associated with formal sexual harassment charges. *Personnel Psychology, 38*, 559–574.

Browne, K. R. (2002). *Biology at work: Rethinking sexual equality*. New Brunswick, NJ: Rutgers University Press.

Browne, K. R. (2010). The evolutionary psychology of sexual harassment. In J.D. Duntley & T. K. Shackelford (Eds.), *Evolutionary forensic psychology* (pp. 81–100). New York: Oxford University Press.

Kennair, L. E. O., & Bendixen, M. (2012). Sociosexuality as predictor of sexual harassment and coercion in female and male high school students. *Evolution and Human Behavior, 33* (5), 479–490.

Bendixen, M., & Kennair, L. E. O. (2017). Advances in the understanding of same-sex and opposite-sex sexual harassment. *Evolution and Human Behavior, 38* (5), 583–591.

Zeigler-Hill, V., Besser, A., Morag, J., & Campbell, W. K. (2016). The Dark Triad and sexual harassment proclivity. *Personality and Individual Differences, 89*, 47–54.

Gutek, B. A. (1985). *Sex and the workplace: The impact of sexual behavior and harassment on women, men, and the organization.* San Francisco, CA: Jossey-Bass.

Buss, D. M. (2016b). *The evolution of desire: Strategies of human mating (revised and updated edition).* New York: Basic Books.

Studd, M. V., & Gattiker, U. E. (1991). The evolutionary psychology of sexual harassment in organizations. *Ethology and Sociobiology, 12*, 249–290.

Colarelli, S. M., & Haaland, S. (2002). Perceptions of sexual harassment: An evolutionary perspective. Psychology, *Evolution, and Gender, 4*, 243–264.

DeSouza, E. R., Pierce, T., Zanelli, J. C., & Hutz, C. (1992). Perceived sexual intent in the U.S. and Brazil as a function of nature of encounter, subjects' nationality, and gender. *Journal of Sex Research, 29*, 251–260.

Bendixen, M. (2014). Evidence of systematic bias in sexual over-and underperception of naturally occurring events: A direct replication of in a more gender-equal culture. *Evolutionary Psychology, 12* (5), 1004–1021.

Browne, K. R. (2006). Sex, power, and dominance: The evolutionary psychology of sexual harassment. *Managerial and Decision Economics, 27*, 145–158.

Wilson, M., & Daly, M. (1996). Male sexual proprietariness and violence against wives. *Current Directions in Psychological Science, 5*, 2–7.

Cousins, A. J., & Gangestad, S. W. (2007). Perceived threats of female infidelity, male proprietariness, and violence in college dating couples. *Violence and Victims, 22*, 651–668.

Kaighobadi, F., & Shackelford, T. K. (2009). Suspicions of female infidelity predict men's partner-directed violence. *Behavioral and Brain Sciences, 32*, 281–282.

Buss, D. M., & Duntley, J. D. (2011). The evolution of intimate partner violence. *Aggression and Violent Behavior, 16* (5), 411–419.

Shackelford, T. K., Goetz, A. T., Buss, D. M., Euler, H. A., & Hoier, S. (2005). When we hurt the ones we love: Predicting violence against women from men's mate retention. *Personal Relationships, 12*, 447–463.

Wilson, M., & Daly, M. (1993). An evolutionary psychological perspective on male sexual proprietariness and violence against wives. *Violence and Victims, 8*, 271–294.

Belluck, P. (1997, March 31). *A woman's killer is likely to be her partner, a study finds.* New York Times.

Jones, D. N., & De Roos, M. S. (2017). Machiavellian flexibility in negative mate retention. *Personal Relationships, 24* (2), 265–279.

Brewer, G., Hunt, D., James, G., & Abell, L. (2015). Dark Triad traits, infidelity and romantic revenge. *Personality and Individual Differences, 83*, 122–127.

Sela, Y., Shackelford, T. K., Pham, M. N., and Zeigler-Hill, V. (2015). Women's mate retention behaviors, personality traits, and fellatio. *Personality and Individual Differences, 85*, 187–191.

Published by Lulu Press, Inc
627 Davis Drive Suite 300
Morrisville, NC 27560
United States

+1 844 212 0689
www.lulu.com

ISBN: 978-1-716-04863-0